MAC BRIDGES /

IN MY FEELS

HOW TO FEEL GOD WHEN I'M NOT FEELING IT

Published by Lifeway Press® • © 2022 Mac Bridges and Kenz Durham
Reprinted Nov. 2022, Mar. 2023, June 2023, Oct. 2023, Jan. 2024

ISBN: 978-1-0877-6514-3
Item: 005837769

Dewey decimal classification: 152.4
Subject heading: EMOTIONS / ATTITUDE (PSYCHOLOGY) / WOMEN

Unless otherwise noted, all Scripture quotations are taken from the Christian Standard Bible®, Copyright © 2017 by Holman Bible Publishers. Used by permission. Christian Standard Bible® and CSB® are federally registered trademarks of Holman Bible Publishers. Scripture quotations marked (NIV) are taken from the Holy Bible, New International Version®, NIV®. Copyright © 1973, 1978, 1984, 2011 by Biblica, Inc.® Used by permission of Zondervan. All rights reserved worldwide. www.zondervan.com The "NIV" and "New International Version" are trademarks registered in the United States Patent and Trademark Office by Biblica, Inc.® Scripture quotations marked (ESV) are from the ESV® Bible (The Holy Bible, English Standard Version®), copyright © 2001 by Crossway, a publishing ministry of Good News Publishers. Used by permission. All rights reserved.

The Gift of Feelings Chart™ and The Eight Feelings™ used courtesy of Chip Dodd and Sage Hill Counseling.

To order additional copies of this resource, write Lifeway Resources Customer Service; 200 Powell Place, Suite 100, Brentwood, TN 37027; Fax order to 615.251.5933; call toll-free 800.458.2772; email orderentry@lifeway.com; or order online at lifeway.com.

Printed in the United States of America.

Lifeway Girls
Lifeway Resources
200 Powell Place, Suite 100
Brentwood, TN 37027

Editorial Team,
Lifeway Girls
Bible Studies

Ben Trueblood
Director,
Lifeway Students

John Paul Basham
Manager

Karen Daniel
Team Leader

Amanda Mejias
Content Editor

Morgan Hawk
Production Editor

Shiloh Stufflebeam
Graphic Designer

Table of Contents

04 ABOUT THE AUTHORS

08 HOW TO USE

10 WEEK 1
When I'm Feeling Hurt

28 WEEK 2
When I'm Feeling Lonely

46 WEEK 3
When I'm Feeling Sad

64 WEEK 4
When I'm Feeling Angry

82 WEEK 5
When I'm Feeling Afraid

100 WEEK 6
When I'm Feeling Ashamed

118 WEEK 7
When I'm Feeling Guilty

136 WEEK 8
When I'm Feeling Joyful

154 LEADER GUIDE

156 SOURCES

About the Authors

Mac Bridges

Kenz Durham

Hiiiii, we're Mac and Kenz, the voices behind this book. We are best friends, kingdom dreamers, and probably a lot like you. We are so honored to be the ones taking you on this journey all about your feelings. Throughout this book, we will be sharing personal stories and diving into Scripture with you.

Mac Bridges is an ex-country singer from a small town in North Carolina. You probably have the wrong impression of her already because she dresses more like Beyoncé and you'll never catch her with a guitar. On the real tho, she's an incredible speaker and leader. She will fire truth at you even when you aren't ready to hear it. She's confident, strong-willed, and loyal. Just picture a Golden Retriever and pit bull mutt, and you've got Mac!

Kenz Durham is everybody's best friend, ultimate hype girl, and prayer warrior. If you ever meet her, be sure to ask her to show you her speed walk—it's very impressive. Even though she's not a touchy-feely hugger, she always makes sure that everyone in the room feels included and seen. Don't be surprised by her savvy business skills and her ability to bring the house down with a fire prayer. And she is sure to bring a good time no matter where she goes.

Our Core Values

ROOTED IN SCRIPTURE

All of our content is inspired by the Word of God. We believe in having an active and alive relationship with Scripture in our everyday lives. All of our resources and content reflect that heartbeat and come from Jesus-centered truth rooted in Scripture.

FUN & RELATABLE

This isn't your Mom's boring Bible study. (Sorry, Mom!) We strive to create content that meets you right where you are in life. While we don't shy away from the hard stuff, we also don't shy away from almost peeing our pants on the daily from laughing so hard. After all, following Jesus is fun and full of joy!

NOT AFRAID OF HARD TRUTH

We're not afraid to say it like it is and to bring you the HARD truth that you sometimes won't want to hear. We believe wholeheartedly that while conviction, sacrifice, and pruning isn't always easy, it's always worth it in the end when you start to look more and more like Jesus.

NOTE FROM MAC & KENZ

WHY A STUDY ON FEELINGS?

Okay, okay, okay, we've got to start off this study with an honest confession. Why a study on feelings? Well, to be totally frank, Kenz and I were tired of hearing girls obsess over their feelings.

Yep, that's right! We wish it was a better story, but we try to keep it real around here. We've been working in college ministry for the last ten years and can't even begin to count the number of conversations, coffee dates, and late night phone calls we've received from girls all up in their feels. From heartbreak and breakups to anxiety and busy schedules to loneliness and missing home. The list goes on and on!

We are far more comfortable with our feelings than many of the generations that came before us. This is such a good and beautiful thing! We know about words like depression and anxiety. We're comfortable with therapy, and we've learned how to be more vulnerable with our communities. But in a lot of ways, like a pendulum, we've swung to the other side and allowed these feelings to start defining and telling us who we are more than our God. And, unfortunately, it also seems as if following Jesus has become less about who God is and more about how we feel or don't feel about Him on a particular day.

But feelings were never meant to be ignored, suppressed, or pushed aside. We don't have to be ashamed of them. They are a crucial part of walking with Jesus because they actually reveal what's going on inside of us, and through our feelings, we receive a direct invitation from Jesus to experience more of Him.

Join us on a journey of getting in our feels together. We're going to dive into eight core feelings—hurt, loneliness, sadness, anger, fear, shame, guilt, and joy—and see how Scripture highlights the beauty of each one. Our prayer is that this study helps you to better understand and embrace your feelings, while also knowing the truth that even when you don't feel it, God is still inviting you to encounter the richness of His loving kindness.

So grab your girlfriends, tissues, and waterproof mascara—it's time to get in our feels!

EIGHT CORE FEELINGS

SOUR SIDE	CORE FEELING	THE INVITATION
Resentment	Hurt	Healing
Apathy	Lonely	Intimacy
Self-pity	Sad	Embrace
Bitterness	Anger	Passion
Anxiety	Fear	Faith
Self-rejection	Shame	Humility
Pride	Guilt	Freedom
Cheap Pleasure	Joy	Full Life

How to Use

Throughout our eight weeks together, we are going to learn about eight core feelings and the invitation God offers when we are all up in our feels.

> **Hurt, Lonely, Sad, Anger, Fear, Shame, Guilt, Joy**

This is a study that you can do on your own, with your BFF, a group from church, or even some friends you just met. To help make it easy for you, we have broken down each of the eight weeks into three parts.

THE INTRO

Before you start each week, we want you to check out our podcast to introduce the core feeling. All you have to do to get started is scan the QR code and begin streaming. Even though we know that podcasts can be listened to in the car, on a run, or while you're doing homework, we hope you'll take some time to write down any notes you want to hold onto for the week about the feeling we address.

PERSONAL STUDY DAYS

Each week has three personal study days where we get REAL about the core feeling and point you to the invitation God offers us in our feels through God's Word. This is where you want to get vulnerable about what feelings you are dealing with, what feelings you didn't even know you had, and what steps you believe God wants you take.

As you read, you will have prompts that will cause you to answer questions, reflect on where you are, and pray about those feelings. Most importantly, we have designed these Personal Study Days for you to dig deep in God's Word and discover truth for yourself, so make sure you have your Bibles ready to go. If you're doing this with a friend or group, feel free to keep each other accountable even as you work independently each week

GROUP TIME

We can't recommend doing this Bible study alongside other people enough. As you finish getting real with God in your three days of Personal Study, we invite you to get real with those doing this study with you. We know it can feel so awkward to talk about our feelings, but what would we miss out on if we didn't have community to hold us accountable and point us back to truth?

As you can see below, each Group Time will cover four important parts you don't want to miss: Open It Up, Let's Get Real, Living Into the Invitation, and Giving the Invitation. Because we don't want you to just to fill your heads with knowledge and move on, we want God's truth to transform your hearts and move you towards action.

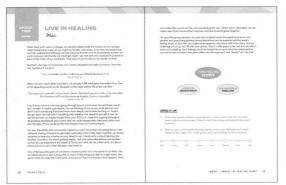

We are so excited for you to get started!

WANT TO START A GROUP TO DO THIS BIBLE STUDY ALONGSIDE? YAY! CHECK OUT OUR LEADER GUIDE ON PAGE 154 TO GET STARTED.

WHEN I'M FEELING HURT

WEEK 1

LISTEN

Kick off this study by streaming our first podcast episode—*When I'm Feeling Hurt*. To get started, all you have to do is scan this QR code and begin streaming. ⋯⋯⋯⋯⋯⋯⋯⋯⋯⋯⋯⋯⋯⋯⋯⋯⋯▶

In this episode, we get real about moments of hurt from our own life, how in the past we've stuffed those feelings, how at times we've allowed ourselves to feel those feelings with Jesus, and what we're learning from Scripture about how to process hurt.

Use the space below to take notes of key points, quotes, and anything else you want to remember from this podcast episode.

THE CORE FEELING: HURT

Kenz

Hurt.

It's that lump in your throat. You know that feeling mid-conversation with someone when you can feel the emotions start to build. The lump gets bigger and bigger to the point that it becomes difficult to swallow. If they were to ask you one more question, it would be a guaranteed outburst of tears.

Hurt is that ache in your chest. The world feels like it stops spinning and it's almost as if the blood physically rushes out of your body. You grab your heart in hopes that it will relieve the pain, but it keeps throbbing.

Hurt is the tears glossing over your eyes. You try to hold them back by blinking a few times and wiping the first few that fall. But without permission, water begins to run down your cheeks, and all of a sudden, you find yourself ugly crying across the table.

That lump, the ache, those tears are all little sirens going off letting you know that you're not okay—something or someone has left you in pain.

Maybe it was a boy that broke up with you, maybe it was a friend that let you down, maybe it was the invite you didn't get, a parent that abandoned you, or the rejection you felt when you didn't get the role of your dreams.

Hurt stings. It runs deep. It doesn't heal on its own. It continuously resurfaces.

When was the last time you can remember experiencing hurt? What hurt you?

The truth is we ALL experience hurt but express it differently.

Some of us are "stuffers." If you are reluctant to read the chapter because you feel like "you don't really get hurt often," you're probably a stuffer. There have most likely been some pretty painful moments in your past, but you've pushed them down—maybe so far down that you're completely ignorant of them at this point. You're good at "sucking it up," moving on, and truthfully a bit prideful in the way you don't care what other people think.

Mac would admit that she is a recovering stuffer. We've been friends for about ten years, and at this point, I can catch her stuffing. Her eyes glaze over, her sentences get shorter, and she says the words, "I don't want to talk about it," avoiding any tears or the explosion of emotion that comes after stuffing.

I think her stuffing habits probably stem from her childhood. As the youngest of four kids, her older siblings used to make fun of her for being "sooooooo sensitive." (Lol, anybody else grow up with older siblings?) Eventually, she trained herself to be "tough" and to suffocate any feelings to try to prove to them that she wasn't a baby. She got used to avoiding her feelings and even started labeling them as weaknesses. She'd admit there are about a thousand times where she said, "I'm doing great," rather than acknowledging her hurt.

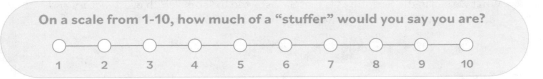

On a scale from 1-10, how much of a "stuffer" would you say you are?

1 2 3 4 5 6 7 8 9 10

Then others of us are "feelers." You might be a feeler if you are known for your tears. Sad tears, happy tears, angry tears, and overall just lots of tears. Feelers might even shamelessly tell people about the latest thing they learned in therapy.

But if you're being honest about being a feeler, there have probably been a few times when you've gotten a little too stuck in your feelings and it turned into self-centeredness. After overthinking everything and replaying conversations countlessly, you have likely had moments where you've feel stuck in your feelings.

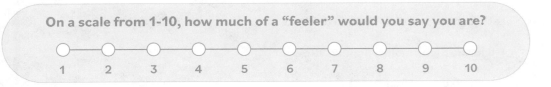

On a scale from 1-10, how much of a "feeler" would you say you are?

1 2 3 4 5 6 7 8 9 10

I personally find myself somewhere in the middle. You better bet I have a good cry every once in a while, but my tears aren't sweet and pretty. Mine are full-on snotty, puffy, obviously "left my emotions undealt with for too long" tears. I will stuff my hurt for awhile, but eventually, the tears fall because I don't have that same endurance of a true "stuffer."

One of the best stuffer/feeler dynamics in all of Scripture is the juxtaposition between Saul and David showcased in 1 Samuel.

Jot down a few things you know about these two kings before we jump in. (Don't know anything yet? No worries, you're about to!)

Saul was king over the Israelites for about twenty years, most of which is documented throughout the first half of 1 Samuel. To be honest, he didn't do a great job and disobeyed the Lord MANY times. Eventually, the Lord appoints a new king, King David. For Saul, it felt like a real stab in the back because David was a lowly farm boy, a couple feet shorter, and outwardly unequipped for the role in comparison to Saul.

Right off the bat, David made Saul look pretty bad. David was killing it on the battlefield, secured many victories, had lots of new fan girls, and things were looking great for him. What we see in the Scriptures is that Saul started to "stuff." With every victory and accolade that David acquired, Saul grew more and more hurt.

Stop and read 1 Samuel 18:6-9.

Just before this passage of Scripture in 1 Samuel 17, you read about David's first big victory against Goliath. You're probably familiar with this story. Goliath was giant, armed, well-trained, and David had no business going up against him. But by the grace of God he won, killing Goliath with a slingshot and stone. Pretty impressive, right?

Now the Israelite army was on their way home, and the women welcomed them home with singing and praise.

What were they singing (v. 7)?

Let's just say Saul didn't handle that well!

Fill in the blank from 1 Samuel 18:9:

"So Saul watched David _____ from that day forward."

I don't know about you, but I can relate to the guy. It's tough when you feel overlooked, when someone is totally showing you up, or gets the spotlight you wanted. Gosh, it hurts!

Can you relate to Saul's bitterness in this passage? What does it remind you of in your own life?

Don't you kind of wish that Saul could have had a vulnerable moment with David?

What do you think Saul would've said to David if he had just been honest and vulnerable about what he was feeling?

Meanwhile, David, our other king, was all up in his feels. As any good creative or musician does, he wrote songs and poems all about his emotions, especially the hurt he faced. People lied to him, dismissed him, and turned their backs on him. David wrote many of the psalms we read today in the midst of this pain as an expression of hurt.

Stop and read Psalm 109. Notice how David came face-to-face with his hurt.

What verse stood out to you?

Psalm 109 was written out of David's pain and hurt from an enemy. It's possible this was written out of the hurt he was experiencing directly from Saul, but we don't know for sure. What we do know is who David focused and directed his hurt and pain to.[1]

How does David's prayer teach you to be more honest with your prayers?

The reality is life is hard and it hurts. You'll never be able to escape that on earth. But the beautiful thing that David teaches us is that these feelings can lead us closer to our Father, rather than simply stuffing our feelings and growing more bitter.

God is our Helper, our Comforter, our Redeemer, our Savior. He came for moments like this. He wants to be a part of your pain, and He will sit there with you in your feelings.

If you haven't listened to this week's podcast, make sure to go back to page 11 to join Mac and me for a conversation all about hurt.

THE SOUR SIDE: RESENTMENT

Kenz

I'll never forget walking into my first ever internship at a church in Nashville, Tennessee. I was a bundle of excitement, and I was dressed to match my confidence. I had on a cute pink dress, white sneakers, and a brand new Target bag to look as if I don't usually miraculously carry my computer, journal, Bible, pens, keys, wallet, water bottle, and coffee all in two hands. After anxiously searching for the correct parking spot, I popped out of my little white sedan and headed down the stairs.

What happened after that was the most humbling experience of my life. I think I must have only made it down the first two steps when I found my entire body sprawled out on the ground, along with everything else in that cute new Target bag. Not only was this extremely embarrassing, but I was legitimately convinced I had broken my leg right there on the stairs.

Turns out I had only sprained my ankle, which basically meant I had to keep moving along. There wasn't a giant cast to signify my pain; I really didn't have a big enough excuse to miss work, stay at home, and chill out for a while.

Doesn't that feel like emotional hurt too? Although you might be hurting, you keep moving, and honestly, no one really cares. And because no one acknowledges it, it's easier to ignore.

It probably sounds a lot like this:

Circle the statement that feels most familiar to you.

"I'm fine."   *"I shouldn't feel this way."*

"It's really not a big deal."   *"It's whatever."*

"Seriously, it's all good."   *"I'm sure I'll get over it."*

Turns out, just as a sprained ankle worsens as you ignore it, your emotional pain does as well. That once invisible swelling starts to turn an ugly greenish-blue, and you cannot hide it any more. The pain doesn't go away—it only gets more painful.

What typically holds you back from expressing or admitting your pain?

The result of ignoring, stuffing, avoiding, denying, minimizing, heck whatever you do to cover your pain, turns into the sour side of hurt: *resentment*.

Why is it that a word none of us need to google to know what it means?

I've resented . . .
+ That mean girl at school who never once invited me to her birthday party.
+ That popular girl with the personality I wished I had.
+ That guy I had a crush on who could never remember my name.

Maybe for you, you've resented . . .
+ That friend who left you in the dust to join the cool crowd.
+ That teacher who never gave you affirmation despite your straight As.
+ That parent who was too busy at work to notice your tears.

When's the last time you remember feeling resentment toward someone? What did you resent them for?

There's this moment in Scripture that gives us a pretty real picture of resentment, so real it might make you cringe a little bit. Today we're going to look at a story in Genesis 37 and some good 'ole family drama because of a guy named Joseph.

If you grew up going to Sunday School, you might be familiar with Joseph's story and his fancy-smancy coat of many colors. Before we jump in, you're going to need to know a little more about his family line.

Joseph's parents were Jacob and Rachel. Joseph's father had another wife named Leah, but he loved Rachel a lot more. Leah had many sons with Jacob, all the while Rachel struggled having just one child. After years of being angry at God, the Lord finally gave her a son named Joseph. So Joseph was the long-awaited, golden child, and let's just say that his brothers weren't too happy about it.

Stop and read Genesis 37:1-4.

What do you pick up on in these first four verses?

These first few verses emphasize the fact that Joseph was Jacob's favorite. He gifted Joseph a "long-sleeved robe" as an outward display of his love for him. This was that coat of many colors that you might've heard of before. It signified "a position of favor, princely standing, and birthright."[2]

Stop and read Genesis 37:4 again.

So what did Joseph's brothers think about the favoritism that was taking place? Well, they hated him for it—to the point they couldn't even bring themselves to speak to him.

Have you ever been there before? Resentment has built up so much in your heart toward a friend, your mom, boyfriend, or roommate that you can barely even talk to them.

Have you ever avoided or ran away from a conversation you know you should've had because of resentment? What was that situation?

That's exactly what Joseph's brothers did. They started to avoid him all together, and guess what? Their resentment grew stronger!

As we keep reading in Genesis, we find that Joseph ended up having a few interesting dreams that he decided to loop his family in on.

Stop and read Genesis 37:5-10.

As I'm sure you could have guessed, this made his brothers hate him even more. Like what? You're going to rule over us, and we're going to serve you? Psh, give us a break!

As you keep reading, his brother's jealousy gets worse and worse until eventually . . .

Read Genesis 37:19-20.

Joseph's brothers decided they were going to throw him into a pit where the wild animals would eat him. Yikes! Thankfully, Reuben, the oldest brother, convinced them that it'd be way better to sell him into slavery than murder him themselves.

Now, before you are left with a terrible impression of Joseph's brothers and dislike them forever, take a moment to look a little closer at the text. On the surface they look mean, resentful, and just plain awful. But what if they were just really hurt?

Where could Joseph's brothers hurt be coming from?

They felt overlooked and less than. Let's start with the fact that their dad bought Joseph the most obnoxiously amazing coat. I doubt his brothers felt loved and chosen by Jacob in the same way that Joseph felt.

And not only do I think they were overlooked by their earthly father, but I have a feeling that they felt that way about their heavenly Father too. Don't you think they wished the Lord had given them each a dream and a great calling just like He did for Joseph?

They felt helpless. Genesis 37:2 says that Joseph was seventeen when his brothers finally exploded with resentment and sold him into slavery. For seventeen whole years his brothers stuffed their pain while their jealousy grew and grew.

Can you imagine what would happen if these guys walked into a therapist's office? They would swing open that door and with all the angst in the world blurt out: "Our brother is messed up! He walks around with this obnoxious coat on, and now he's telling us we're going to bow down to him!"

The therapist, probably noticing their resentment, might ask, "Why does this make you so mad?"

"Well, he's saying we're going to BOW DOWN to him, and he thinks he's entitled because his mom is Jacob's favorite. He thinks he hears from God more than the rest of us and . . . "

The therapist would probably softly interpret them to ask the simple but gruesomely direct question, "Do you feel hurt by your dad?"

The lump begins to build in their throats, the ache sharpens in their chests, and the tears start to bubble over their eyes. The years of stuffing, pretending, and ignoring all the pain begins to wash away as they start to get real about their hurt and let God in to work.

As we close out today's reading, I challenge you to peel back the layers of resentment. I wonder what hurt is perhaps buried deep under your resentment.

What hurt and resentment have you stored up in your heart? Why have you been hesitant to open up about it before now?

Hear me clearly: there's always something you can do with your hurt. You don't have to let it control you. You don't have to let it ruin your relationships. You don't have to hide it or wear it everywhere you go. You have a personal invitation to get super honest about your pain and bring it to the feet of Jesus.

Who's ready to learn how to give your hurt to Jesus? (Circle one.)

AHH IDK! ●————● NERVOUS, BUT READY! ●————● LET'S DO THE THING!

THE INVITATION: HEALING

Mac

Over the past few days, we've been talking about what it's like to feel the ache, sting, and sharp pains of hurt. We all have our own stories from the past of hurtful moments and even current situations that we're in the midst of processing through.

But have you ever wondered if Jesus's heart ever hurt? Did He ever feel the knot in His stomach or the ache in His chest? And if He did—how did He respond to the people who wounded Him emotionally?

If you grew up in or around church, you're more than likely aware of Jesus's divine nature. You know that He could heal the sick with one touch, abstain from all sins, walk on water, calm the storms, and even defeat death.

But isn't it also amazing to think that Jesus wasn't just fully God, He was also fully man? He knew what it was like to walk in the brokenness of our world, to come face-to-face with temptation, while feeling the full spectrum of human emotions. Jesus felt what you feel today!

Read Hebrews 4:14-15.

When Jesus became "God with us" (Matt. 1:23) on earth, Jesus got in the mess of it all and took on the fullness of life even as God. He knows the temptations, the pain, and the hurt you feel because He has felt it all Himself as a human on earth. He isn't far removed from you when you face temptation, get caught in your feelings, and experience deep hurt. Instead, Jesus is right there with you in it all.

Yesterday, we looked at the sour side of hurt, how when left unattended, it often turns into resentment. Today we're going to look at how not to ignore it, but what to actually do with the hurt that we feel.

What invitation do you think Jesus offers you when you look to Him to care for your hurting heart?

Scripture shows us that Jesus in His loving kindness invites us into *healing*.

One of Jesus's most loyal companions was a zealous, bold, and sometimes prideful guy named Peter. Once a failed fisherman turned into a "fisher of men" (Matt. 4:19), Peter seemed not only to have made it into Jesus's inner circle as one of the disciples but a beloved friend of Jesus.

On the night that Jesus was taken into custody by the Romans, Jesus shared a final meal with His disciples known as the last supper. Afterwards, they made a short journey outside of Jerusalem to a place called the Mount of Olives. In that place, Jesus shared that many of them would abandon Him that very night.

Turn to Matthew 26 and read verses 30-35.

Which one of Jesus's disciples declared this, "Even if everyone falls away because of you, I will never fall away" (v. 33)?

How did Jesus respond (v. 34)?

Peter refused to admit that he would ever turn his back on Jesus despite the fact that Jesus straight-up told him that before that very night was over, Peter would disown Him not once, but three times. In verse 35, Peter denied it again. There was just no way he would ever hurt Jesus! (Spoiler alert: he was wrong.)

Flip to Matthew 26 and read verses 69-75.

How many times did Peter deny Jesus?

That's right. Peter denied Jesus three times. And just as the rooster crowed, Peter remembered that this was exactly what Jesus had predicted would happen. Peter, despite his best efforts and hopes, had betrayed his Lord, the One he swore he would never hurt in a million years. He had completely and totally left Jesus in His darkest and hardest moment. I wonder how Jesus must've felt knowing that Peter would deny Him.

How do you think YOU would feel if your closest friend betrayed you not once, but THREE times?

| It's totally fine! | Bummed, but you would forgive her. | I'm totally unaffected. | She better BEG for your forgiveness! | Girlllll, it's over! |

If Kenz, my best friend in the entire world, denied knowing me three times, I know I would be extremely hurt. I mean, how could she do that to me? What happened to all those years of friendship? What about all the promises she made to me?

How do you typically respond when someone hurts you?

Jesus, unlike me and probably unlike you, had a different response.

In Mark 16, we read about several women who went to visit the tomb of Jesus after His death on the cross. When they arrived at the tomb, the stone covering the entrance was rolled away. Upon entering the tomb, they found an angel there who delivered the good news that Jesus was indeed alive. Then, he gave them a few specific instructions.

Stop and read Mark 16:7.

Okay, hold up! Jesus had just been betrayed by His friends, suffered a painful death, rose from the grave, defeated sin and death, and one of the first things on His "to-do list" was to have an angel set up a meeting place for Him to reconcile with Peter? Like what?! This is not the way my human heart would respond. No joke, I once gave my sister the silent treatment for an entire week because she ate my leftovers.

John 21 recounts the powerful moment of reconciliation when Jesus drew Peter back to Himself through a moment of deep spiritual healing. Spend some time reading this passage of Scripture. Look for how Jesus calls Peter into healing.

Stop and read John 21:1-19.

How many times does Jesus ask Peter about his love for Him (vv. 15-17)? Why does that number sound familiar?

Yes! Each confession covered one of Peter's three denials. He had to come face-to-face with his failures. But instead of punishment or making him feel guilty for what he had done, each time Jesus responded simply with "feed my sheep."

Jesus told Peter that despite the pain he had caused, His calling remained the same. His failures didn't bench him or take him out of the game. Jesus still wanted Peter and still wanted to use him. I can only imagine the deep healing that Peter found in that moment with Jesus. It's almost as if Jesus was able to use His deepest hurt to tee up His deepest healing.

Because when hurt is dealt with in a healthy way, it moves the heart toward healing.

Let's look at one more passage of Scripture together. Keep in mind that these words come from a letter written by none other than our beloved disciple, Peter.

Flip to 1 Peter 2:24 and fill in the blanks below:

"He himself bore our sins in his body on the tree; so that, having died to sins, we might live for righteousness. By his _____ you have been _____."

By His wounds you have been healed.

Let that sink in for a moment. Jesus went to the cross for your healing.

Do you believe that?

| There's just no way! | I want to, but my heart is too broken. | Ehhhhh, maybe on some days. | Yes, but I still have a few doubts. | 1,000% |

I wonder if Peter wasn't thinking back to how Jesus had changed everything and offered him new life through those three powerful questions after His death and resurrection as he was writing. Despite feeling the feels of His own hurt and pain, Jesus offered Peter complete healing through what He did on the cross.

When we are deeply hurting, whether from our own doing or not, Jesus offers us that same healing. When you are facing the deepest kind of pain that you think nobody in the world could possibly understand, Jesus gets it. He knows what it's like to be betrayed. He knows what it's like to be rejected. He knows what it's like for your heart to ache. Jesus bore the weight of all our sin, hurt, and pain on His shoulders when He hung on that cross.

Jesus did that so that you and I could have somewhere to turn when we're hurting. He bore it all so we could receive His beautiful invitation into a relationship with Him that leads to healing and restoration.

Be honest. Have you brought your hurt to the Lord and genuinely asked for healing? What's keeping you from accepting Jesus's invitation to healing?

You don't have to ignore the hurt you're currently feeling. You don't have to tie it up with a pretty bow. You don't even have to dry your tears. You simply have to take that hurt to the feet of Jesus and reach out your hands to be healed in His loving arms. By His wounds, you will be healed.

LIVE IN HEALING
Mac

When Kenz and I were in college, we started a Bible study for women on our campus called Delight that some of you might be familiar with today. From the very beginning, we both realized that although we had amazing friends who we loved being around, we were missing a community we could get super real with and who could point us back to Jesus in the midst of our hardships. That type of community is a lot harder to find!

But that's the type of community our Creator designed and calls us to be in. I love the way Galatians 6:2 puts it:

> *"Carry one another's burdens; in this way you will fulfill the law of Christ."*
> GALATIANS 6:2

When we carry each other's burdens, we actually fulfill what Jesus has asked of us. One of His departing words to His disciples on the night before His arrest was this:

> *"I give you a new command: Love one another. Just as I have loved you, you are also to love one another. By this everyone will know that you are my disciples, if you love one another."*
> JOHN 13:34-35

I don't know what or who was going through Jesus's mind when He said these words, but I wonder if maybe, just maybe, He was thinking of you as you sit all alone in your dorm room wondering if anyone knows how deeply you've been hurting, or maybe the girl down the hall who's wrestling with whether she needs to just get in her car and drive home, or maybe the girl from your 8:00 a.m. class who is going through a devastating heartbreak. Jesus knew that we would desperately need each other and that His type of love would be the only thing to heal our hurting hearts.

You see, friendship and community is about so much more than not sitting alone in the cafeteria, having someone to get ready with before the Friday night mayhem, or having someone to help you scheme on your latest crush. Community is about bearing one another's burdens. It's about getting messy, real, and vulnerable before one another so that we can experience the depth of Christ and what He has called us to. It's about showing love to each other like Jesus has loved us.

One of the beautiful parts of emotions is knowing that we're not alone in our feels. Like we talked about on Day 3, Jesus felt so many of the things you feel on a daily basis, and guess what? So does the community around you! There's a freedom that happens when you realize that you're not the only one feeling this way. When we're vulnerable, we can relate, learn from one another's stories, and look towards Jesus together.

For your first group session, we want you to spend some time getting to know one another and practicing getting honest about how you've experienced this week's feeling (hurt) in your life. You might be tempted to only share half of the story, but we challenge you to go ALL IN with your group. This is a safe space to be real and raw about what you're feeling. Your feelings won't be looked down upon here but celebrated as you look to the invitation that Jesus offers you through each one. Ready? Let's do this!

OPEN IT UP:

1. **Grab your phone and look through your camera roll until you find your most embarrassing photo. Share it with the group and explain the story behind it.**

2. **Start to get comfortable sharing openly about your feelings each week. Which of the eight core feelings are you most feeling at this moment?**

LET'S GET REAL:

1. On Day 1, we talked about the difference between "stuffers" and "feelers." Rank yourself on a scale from 1 to 10 (1 meaning you are the ultimate stuffer; 10 meaning you are always up in your feels). Why did you score yourself that way?

2. What's the deepest hurt you're currently feeling in your life? What have you been doing with your hurt? Has this hurt started to morph into resentment? How so?

LIVING INTO THE INVITATION:

The second that Peter saw Jesus on the shore he got off the boat and swam as fast as he could to Jesus (John 21:7). He knew that he needed healing and didn't want to miss this moment of reconciliation with Jesus.

1. What has been keeping you from bringing your hurt to Jesus?

2. What would it look like for you to "schedule a meeting" or have a time of reconciliation/healing with Him? How can your group hold you accountable to this?

GIVING THE INVITATION:

No matter how hurt Jesus might have felt by Peter, He still offered Peter an invitation into healing. Jesus could've let His hurt turn into bitterness and denied Peter reconciliation, but instead He went out of His way to pursue Peter again.

1. **Is there someone in your life that has hurt you that you've been avoiding?**

2. **What would it look like to push past your resentment and offer them an invitation for reconciliation/healing?**

WHEN I'M FEELING LONELY

WEEK 2

LISTEN

As we begin a new week, scan the QR code and join us for a conversation all about loneliness. In this podcast episode, we get real about moments of true loneliness from our own lives, how in the past we've run from these feelings, and what we're learning from Scripture about how to allow loneliness to lead us into deeper relationships moving forward.

THE CORE FEELING: LONELY
Mac

Have you ever been in a crowded room full of people chatting, smiling, and laughing, and still felt utterly and completely lonely? I know I have—probably more times than I'd be willing to admit.

Loneliness has been a defining part of my story throughout many seasons of my life. I felt lonely sitting in the cafeteria my sophomore year of high school after moving to a new town. I remember desperately wishing someone would sit down next to me so I wouldn't look like a total loser.

I felt lonely my first two months of college, laying in my twin bed in my dark dorm room scrolling on my phone wondering if I'd ever find my people like everyone else seemed to have found.

I felt lonely my junior year of college when all my friends decided to start partying on the weekends and I was the only one making the decision not to.

I felt lonely in my apartment off of Hillsboro because, despite having a million "friends," nobody knew the fullness of the internal battle I was facing.

I felt lonely at my best friend's engagement party. I remember looking around at all of the couples and feeling so hopeless as everyone was graduating onto the next season of life. But was I just destined to be the token single girl forever?

When was the last time you felt lonely? What sparked that feeling of loneliness?

The truth is that we all feel lonely in some shape or form. Some of us have a million friends, but we don't feel truly known by anyone. Some of us feel lonely because we feel misunderstood or overlooked. Some of us can't seem to find our "people" or that group that we can always count on to show up when we need them. Some of us are longing for a relationship—that someone we can give our hearts to and build a life with.

The hard part about loneliness is that you can't calculate how lonely you are by counting the number of relationships you have. It can't be cured with a few swipes on a dating app. It can't be defined with a WebMD description. It's often a quiet feeling that haunts even the happiest of moments.

Let's get real! On a scale from 1-10, how lonely do you feel right now?

| 1 | 2 | 3 | 4 | 5 | 6 | 7 | 8 | 9 | 10 |

This week we're going to wrestle with the feeling of loneliness together and look for the invitation that God is offering us when we allow ourselves to feel the fullness of it in the safety of His arms.

Let's start by going back to the beginning and see the very first time that loneliness enters the story of humanity.

Open up your Bible to Genesis 2 and read verses 4-25.

Fill in the blanks from verse 18:

Then the Lord God said, "It is not good for the man to be_____. I will make a _____corresponding to him."

God straight up said that it wasn't good for Adam to be alone! Let's stop and think about the magnitude of this for a moment. When we think of the story of Adam and Eve, we're often quick to jump to the fall. But if we slow down and look closely, I think we see a beautiful piece of God's heart for humanity here that we shouldn't look past.

Before the creation of Eve, Adam walked in a daily, personal, and up close relationship with God. It was just he and God day after day! Imagine waking up and drinking your morning coffee with God, taking a post-work stroll with Him, and ending the night on the couch side-by-side with a hot cup of Sleepytime Tea and an episode of *The Great British Bake Off*. Just you and God! Honestly sounds pretty dreamy, right?

Describe your dream day with just you and God. What would it include? What would you do together?

Okay, I'm loving picturing these dream days with God! But hold up—in verse 18, God Himself says that despite that bliss, there was still something missing.

Adam wasn't meant to be alone. He was created for an intimate relationship with God, but the fullness of God's plan for Adam wouldn't be complete until he was in relationship with others. That's why He created Eve! It was through the power of relationships that God's plan for humanity would be put on display.

You and I were created for relationship—relationship with our Creator AND with our fellow creations. It's through community that the full, beautiful picture of our triune God (Father, Son, and Spirit) and His purpose for creation is displayed.

Don't you love that? You weren't created to be alone. You were created to do life with others!

How does Genesis 2:18 make you feel? (Pick which best describes you.)

    A) Hopeful that God wants that for me.

    B) Confused, but then why am I so lonely?

    C) Grateful for the relationships in my life!

    D) Convicted because I've been neglecting community in my life.

Have you ever felt like God doesn't care about your relationships or your lack of relationships? How does this give you hope for what He wants for you?

I love knowing that God's heart for me is not to be alone, but to be in vibrant, meaningful, and real relationships with the people around me. And this is so beautifully expressed through His Son, Jesus.

Jesus had the most intimately beautiful relationship with God, but during His time walking on earth, He was still all about relationships. He didn't do life alone. He invited people into His inner circle to do life with Him in the sweet and hard times. Like we talked about last week, Jesus wasn't immune to the feelings that we feel. In His humanity, He knew what it was like to feel the deep pangs of loneliness—to desperately need others.

Open up your Bible to Matthew 26. Read verses 36-46.

Who did Jesus take with Him to pray (v. 37)?

What does He ask them to do in verse 38?

Jesus was getting ready to die a painful death on a cross for the sins of the entire world. Can you imagine feeling more lonely than that? Nobody could truly understand or empathize with what He was going through. And Jesus was going to have to do it alone!

I love that Jesus could have done a million things in response to this moment, but how do we see Jesus act in the midst of His intense feelings?

First, He called three of his closest friends to simply be with Him. I'm sure Jesus (you know, the Son of God, Savior of the world, God incarnate) would've been more than okay facing these moments without His friends, yet He still wanted them there with Him. Jesus asking people to be with Him was not a sign of weakness.

When you're feeling alone, do you invite people to be "with you"?

| Literally never! | It's a rare occasion. | I typically keep it to myself. | I'm usually super honest with how I feel! | My people are on speed dial! |

What we see Jesus do next is share openly and honestly about the grief and sorrow He was experiencing. He didn't hide how He was feeling. He was raw and vulnerable before them and even invited them in to help Him by staying and keeping watch. We see in verses 40-46 that they did a terrible job at that, but Jesus, fully knowing they would mess up, found it necessary to include His people.

Finally, we see how Jesus went to God in prayer in the midst of His deep feelings of loneliness and despair.

Complete this verse from Matthew 26:39.

> Going a little farther, he fell _____ and prayed, "My _____, if it is possible, let this cup pass from me. Yet not as I will, but as you will."

Jesus knew that the only One who could fully understand His deepest feelings of loneliness and pain was His Father in heaven. Only God could truly fulfill His deepest needs, so He sought Him by crying out in prayer, not just once but three times.

Jesus perfectly models for us that loneliness isn't a feeling we have to avoid at all costs. Instead, it should move us towards relationship—both in deeper communion with God and with the people God has placed around us.

THE SOUR SIDE: APATHY
Mac

I'll never forget the moment. I was a few months into my freshman year at Belmont University in Nashville, Tennessee. It was Friday night and all day long I had eagerly been checking my phone hoping and praying that someone was going to text me.

Maybe the nice girl with the kind smile who sat next to me in my freshman seminar? Maybe the cute baseball player who was in my orientation group? Maybe the girl who lived three doors down and talked a lot? I mean, I would have even taken my dad's old friend from college who lived twenty minutes away and had given me his number in case of emergency. I seriously considered texting him. This felt like an emergency!

I was two months into college in the city of my dreams and I was sitting alone in my dorm room on a Friday night with no one to hang out with. My roommate was out of town, and I hadn't made friends as quickly as I'd imagined I would.

I heard laughter outside my thin wooden dorm room door as a group of girls from down the hall prepared to head out for the night. I wondered where they were going? How had they connected so quickly? What would they think if they knew I was in here all alone?

I remember tangibly feeling lonely in those moments, but even more so feeling ashamed of my loneliness. I felt like I couldn't tell anyone, call anyone, or ask anyone for help. If I admitted my loneliness, I would be admitting that I wasn't as brave, bold, and strong as I once thought.

So you know what I did? I ate microwavable pizza rolls and oatmeal for forty-eight hours, binged three seasons of *Friday Night Lights*, and didn't leave my room other than to shower in our less than glamorous community bathrooms.

When you're feeling lonely, what other feelings are typically attached to it? (Circle any that apply to you.)

Shame   *Depression*   *Worry*   *Stress*   *Anger*

Apathy   *Disappointment*   *Bitterness*   *Confusion*

Rather than letting my loneliness compel me towards relationships, I let it repel me away from people into a spiral of indifference. I started to convince myself that people couldn't hold power over me if I didn't care about them first. I tried to tell myself that I didn't even want to hang out with anyone (lol). I would've preferred to be alone!

That weekend and in the weeks to come, I became apathetic in my pursuit of community, even though it was the thing I truly wanted most. But the result of running from, ignoring, and/or soaking in loneliness is that it often turns sour and morphs into a defense mechanism called indifference.

Indifference looks like turning off your heart to emotion. It's when you neither like or dislike things, love or hate things—you simply feel nothing.

You find yourself saying . . .
+ Who cares?
+ So what?
+ Ehhhh.
+ It's whatever!

At first, indifference can seem harmless, but it's actually one of the most dangerous emotions for us to dwell in. When you enter into a state of indifference, you attempt to bulletproof your heart to make sure that nothing harmful ever gets in. And you might be able to block out the tears, the pain, and the loneliness, but you also block out the joy, the laughter, and the fulfillment of a beautiful life lived with God and community.

Let's get real! How has indifference been showing up in your life recently?

Today we're going to look at someone from Scripture whose loneliness led him to a state of heartbreaking indifference. Let me introduce you to the prophet Elijah.

Turn to 1 Kings 19 and read verses 1-8. Who was Elijah running away from?

Before we go any further, let me set the scene for what was happening in this tragic moment in Elijah's story. Elijah was a prophet chosen by God to speak on His behalf to the nation of Israel. In the early days, Elijah had a pretty sweet gig! God used him to do all sorts of cool stuff. Things like causing the dew and rain to stop for more than three years (1 King 17:1), resurrecting a woman's son (17:22), and calling down fire from heaven to defeat 450 prophets of Baal (18:37-38).

However, things were not all rainbows and butterflies for Elijah!

During this moment in Israel's history, the nation as a whole had completely turned their backs on God. It was during the reign of King Ahab and Queen Jezebel, and let's just say they weren't the most upstanding leaders.

Fill in the blanks from 1 Kings 16:30:

> But _____ son of Omri did what was _____
> in the Lord's sight more than all who were before him.

Elijah had his work cut out for him, and eventually that pressure and isolation got to him. We see Elijah reach his breaking point in 1 Kings 19. He felt isolated in his beliefs and his convictions. He had convinced himself that he was totally alone in his pursuit of obedience for God. He fled to the desert and plopped down under a broom tree alone, depressed, and an emotional hot mess.

What does Elijah ask God for in verse 4?

He prayed that God would take his life. He had reached the point where his isolation and feelings of being alone had gotten the best of him. Simply put, he just wanted the pain to stop.

Elijah's loneliness had gone sour and indifference was now the posture of his heart. It would've been easier to feel nothing than to feel the heaviness of the emotions he was in the midst of.

Have you ever been there before? Perhaps you've felt so alone and isolated in your feelings that it has crossed your mind to hit the eject button on life and call it quits. Maybe it has felt like nobody could possibly begin to understand the depths of your pain.

Satan uses extreme isolation as a way of whispering nasty lies to us and convincing us of things like:
+ Nobody cares about you.
+ You're always going to be alone.
+ Nobody would care if you were gone.

What lies has Satan been whispering to you while being alone or isolated?

What an evil trick of the enemy. The enemy uses indifference to convince us that it's safer to run away from love and community, while God uses loneliness as a signpost for us to run fast straight toward those things.

Can I challenge you that whenever you next feel lonely (which will happen one day) that you would run toward the Father instead of turning off your heart?

I can promise you that in the hands of God, you will find Him whispering the opposite of the enemy.
+ You are abundantly cared for!
+ You were never alone!
+ Your presence is wanted and needed!

In 1 Kings 19 in the exact moment we see Elijah turning off his heart, God was in radical pursuit of waking it up again. It's beautiful to see how God's response stood in such stark contrast to Elijah's indifference. God in His very nature is never indifferent. He is merciful and always moved to response.

Turn to Ephesians 2 and read verses 4-5 about God's mercy. Fill in the blanks below:

> But God, who is rich in _____, because of his great _____ that he had for us, made us alive with Christ even though we were _____ in trespasses. You are saved by grace!

As we close out today and prepare for tomorrow's study on God's invitation in our loneliness, I want you to finish reading 1 Kings 19:9-18 and look for how God responded in the midst of Elijah's indifference. Take note of His pursuit of Elijah's heart and how He led him toward relationship rather than away from it.

Read 1 Kings 19:9-18.

Take notes here as you read: _____

_____

_____

_____

_____

THE INVITATION: INTIMACY

Kenz

Yesterday, we talked about how undealt loneliness turns into indifference. We stop caring, stay stuck in our loneliness, and feel all together apathetic. Today, we're going to look at how Jesus gives us the invitation into deeper intimacy with Him even on our loneliest days.

Jesus is your best friend. He's the guy you can count on when no one else is there. He will never ditch you, leave you, or turn His back on you. He'll never be fake and will always give you the honest truth. He's a shoulder to cry on, empathic, kind, and caring. You don't have to hold anything back when you're together. He's everything you want in a best friend.

Are you convinced of this?

| Yeah, not about the whole Jesus BFF thing. | Cheesssssssy! | Jesus is truly my best friend! | I want Him to be that for me! |

Well, if you're anything like me, you might low key, (okay, high key) be rolling your eyes at the whole Jesus as your BFF thing. How could a God that can often feels so far away and so mysterious be my best friend? What does that look like? Can He really fill this hole in my heart and satisfy my longing for a relationship?

Scripture shows us that the answer is YES! Jesus is the BEST friend. And rather than slapping this Christian cliché on your forehead, I want to lean in a little closer and see what it truly can look like for Jesus to be your best friend.

Like most real friendships, it begins with intimacy.

What is a friendship in your life that feels the most intimate? What does intimacy in friendship mean to you?

Intimacy occurs when we live in vulnerability, truthfulness, and transparency. It's getting "real real" with each other. Intimacy requires you to honestly open up and surrender to your hard core desire to be known.

I think we can all easily distinguish the difference between a friendship that stays on the surface and one that is intimate. Surface level friendships consist of a lot of "catching up" and getting stuck in a cycle of just hanging out. These friendships might feel comfortable and fill the void of loneliness in your life, but lead you to needing to prove yourself and be liked. It might be fine for a little while, but surface level friendships will slowly dwindle or eventually crash and burn.

On the other hand, intimate friends are in it for the long haul. They break the cycle of needing to prove yourself because you're fully understood. You can be your most authentic, broken, awkward, and messy self, yet they still love you.

Initiating intimacy in friendship can be extremely intimidating at first. But once you make yourself fully known to someone, you'll discover that it's incredibly life-giving and how Jesus always intended it to be.

Now for the real question, does your relationship with Jesus feel intimate?

Have you let Him into the quiet, broken parts of your heart? When you talk to Him, do you stay on the surface or do you go deep? Are there things you hide from Him or do you let Him into the embarrassing, shameful stuff? Do you feel like you have to prove something to Him or do you feel fully loved for just who you are?

There's a moment in Scripture found in Genesis 16 that has always caught my eye. It's an intimate moment where the Lord encountered Hagar, an Egyptian servant, in one of her most broken and desperate places. He met her there, right in the middle of her mess. Let's open up our Bibles and look a little closer.

Stop and read Genesis 16:1-3.

These first few verses tell us that Sarai was having trouble having kids. You can almost hear the pain in her voice as she shared her frustration with Abram (later to be named Abraham). She was upset with God, so she decided to take matters into her own hands.

What does Sarai suggest doing (v. 2)?

She suggested that Abram try to have a child with her servant, Hagar. Of course, this was not the wisest decision. She acted out of distrust and impatience rather than trusting God's timing and plan. But in her sinfulness, she commanded this to happen and Abram agreed to it.

I wish Scripture gave us a little more on Hagar's response in all this. Abram was about to act as a husband and she might become a mom. I'm sure it was the most shocking news of all time!

Stop and read Genesis 16:4-10.

As it turns out, Hagar followed through with the plan and became pregnant. Well, like most poor choices, it didn't turn out so well for either of the women. They began to have some serious "beef" with each other. Sarai became jealous, bitter, and regretful to the point of wrongfully mistreating Hagar.

What does Hagar decide to do (v. 6)?

Out of her despair, Hagar decided to run away from the abusive household. But in her worst and most vulnerable moment, the Lord showed up.

Complete the verse from Genesis 16:7:

> The angel of the LORD _____ _____ by a spring in the wilderness, the spring on the way to Shur.

I love that the Lord found her. He sought her out on her loneliest day when she had no one around her, no one else to turn to, and no one else who cared for her.

I can imagine Hagar was frightened and pretty embarrassed when the Lord appeared to her. She was well aware of the sin she took part in and was probably tempted to cover her belly with her extra cloth and dirty clothes so the Lord wouldn't notice. It was messy. It was raw. It was real. It was vulnerable.

Describe the last time you had an intimate encounter with Jesus.

Let's get real! On a scale from 1-10, how strong is your intimacy with Jesus in this season (1 being not at all; 10 being strongest ever)?

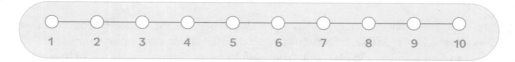

What's crazy about this moment is that this was actually the first time an "angel of the LORD" appeared in the Bible.[1] He didn't first appear to Noah, Enoch, or Abram. He appeared to a single, pregnant, runaway servant in the middle of the desert. He knew she needed Him on her loneliest day.

This is no coincidence; it's very intentional actually. Our God cares! Maybe you've been indifferent and living in hopelessness. Maybe, like Hagar, you are the one that got yourself stuck in this lonely situation. Either way, God will show up for you. But you have to be willing to let Him into the mess.

Scripture goes on to say that the Lord challenged her to go back to Abram and Sarai's home and submit to their authority (v. 9). But through this, He promised to protect her, her son, and their inheritance (v. 10).

Fill in the blanks from Genesis 16:13:

> So she named the LORD who spoke to her: "You are_____," for she said, "In this place, have I actually seen the _____ _____ _____ _____?"

Hagar gave the Lord the name, El-roi which means the "God who sees me." On your loneliest days, when you have no one else to talk to or to love you, God SEES you! He cares. He's there for you. He finds you. He never leaves you.

There's no better friend than Jesus.

Maybe it's time to finally let Him in. Maybe it's time to stop ignoring the desires of your heart and be vulnerable with Him. Maybe it's time for you to stop putting on a show and pretending you are fine. Maybe it's time to stop filling the void with random to-dos and surface level friendships. Just like Hagar, maybe it's time you get intimate with Jesus.

Top of mind, what could this look like for you?

I don't know what it might look like for you, but I do know that you're going to find so much healing and peace in your loneliness when you get intimate with Him. When you let Him into those cracks and crevices of your heart, He's going to speak new life and identity into you. He's going to take care of you, protect you, and love you. He is going to build something beautiful throughout your life.

He is going to be your forever best friend. So will you let Him in?

LIVE IN INTIMACY

Kenz

As we worked through this week's core emotion of loneliness, I hope you recognized how real and prevalent this emotion truly is. You're not going crazy. It's not made up, and it's not just you. When you're feeling lonely, you can know that you're not alone in it.

Not only are there probably a million and a half people around that feel the same way, but there are countless stories in the Bible of both men and women that experienced loneliness too. We've talked about the lonely moments of Jesus Himself, Elijah, and Hagar, but there are even more.

Think about David's loneliness. He spent years in the wilderness trying to escape King Saul who wanted to kill him. Eventually, he made it out of the wilderness and became king. But even on his throne, he dealt with loneliness. He had wealth, fame, many wives, and was the most popular person in Israel, but all of that could not substitute for intimacy with God. You can hear the cry of his heart for connection and belonging all throughout the Psalms.

> *Look to the right and see: no one stands up for me;*
> *there is no refuge for me; no one cares about me.*
> PSALMS 142:4

Think about Jesus's mother, Mary. An angel of the Lord told her she was going to give birth to the Son of God as a virgin when she was only fourteen. Hardly anyone believed her, even her own mother and father abandoned her. She spent all of her life unacknowledged, disconnected from her birth family, and alone.

Think about the bleeding woman in Mark 5. No one wanted to be within feet of her, she couldn't sit with anyone, and if she went out in public, everyone had to know she was unclean. She stayed to herself, isolated, and alone for twelve long years! This woman was so desperate for her loneliness to be healed that she had the courage to go to Jesus and secretly touch the hem of His cloak.

> *"The woman, with fear and trembling, knowing what had happened to her,*
> *came and fell down before him, and told him the whole truth."*
> MARK 5:33

Think about the story of Noah in Genesis 7. God sent a flood that wiped out everyone on the earth but Noah and his family. He spent years of his life in complete isolation.

However, God knew that it was not good for man to be alone, so he rebuilt humanity, friendship, family, and restored the earth. What a sweet reminder that we are not meant to be alone.

You are not alone when you feel lonely! For hundreds and thousands of years, humans have had these same feelings and longings. But there will come a day when we all reach heaven and those earthly feelings and isolation will be gone forever.

Look at what Scripture says here in Revelation:

> *"After this I looked, and there was a vast multitude from every nation, tribe, people, and language, which no one could number, standing before the throne and before the Lamb. They were clothed in white robes with palm branches in their hands. And they cried out in a loud voice: Salvation belongs to our God, who is seated on the throne, and to the Lamb!"*
> REVELATION 7:9-10

I don't know about you, but this gets me excited! In heaven there will be a "vast multitude" of people, so many that Scripture says you wouldn't even be able to count. Now before all the introverts freak out, Scripture also says that we'll simply be looking at our glorious King, our Lord Jesus Christ, and in awe and amazement of Him. We'll be worshiping Him freely and the room will be full of joy. There will be people from all over the world, representing all ethnicities and personalities, and we will be together in unity.

It makes me wonder what it could look like to bring heaven to earth. Although we might not be there yet, I wonder if we could create a heavenly community right here and now. As you move into the group discussion, I want to challenge you to get honest and be more open, to let others in, but most importantly, let Jesus in! Let this be a time when God heals some broken parts of your heart and you experience the healing power of His presence in community.

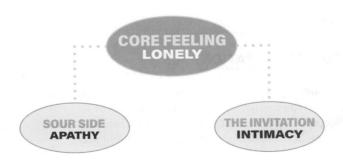

OPEN IT UP:

1. Which of the eight core feelings are you most feeling at this moment?

○———○———○———○———○———○———○———○
Hurt   Lonely   Sad   Anger   Fear   Shame   Guilt   Joy

2. Let's start off this week by sharing one of your most cringy new friend experiences. I think all of us have at least one awkward first friend date!

LET'S GET REAL:

1. How have you been experiencing loneliness recently? Not in the past or an old season, right here and right now!

2. How has indifference been showing up in your life recently? How have you seen it affect your relationships?

LIVING INTO THE INVITATION:

Intimacy with Jesus only happens when you let yourself get intimate with Him. Like Hagar, alone in the desert, caught in the aftermath of sin, shame, and embarrassment, she looked up at the Father and let Him in. It wasn't pretty and put together. It was messy, and broken, and extremely humbling.

1. Have you subtly been avoiding intimacy with Jesus? Why have you not let Him in completely?

2. What do you need to change or do in order to restore intimacy with Him?

GIVING THE INVITATION:

I love the name that Hagar gave to the Lord. She named Him the "God who sees." What if you lived into that name of the Lord this week by noticing others around you that might be hurting or feeling deeply alone in this season. The best way to respond to your loneliness is by putting yourself out there and being the inviter. Everyone loves an invitation, and as simple as it might be, it can be the thing that breaks the cycle of apathy and sadness in someone else's life.

1. Who in your life is experiencing loneliness? How can you be Jesus to them by meeting them in their pain?

2. How can you be the inviter this week? Is there something you can host? People you need to connect?

WHEN I'M FEELING SAD

WEEK 3

LISTEN

As you begin this week, scan the QR code and join us for a conversation all about sadness. In this podcast episode, we talk about our raw and real moments of sadness, the love/hate relationship we have with it, but most importantly, how sadness has drawn us closer to Jesus.

Like any good Bible scholar, I went to YouTube to find the heart wrenching scene from *Air Bud* before writing this chapter. Yep, not the *Passion of the Christ* or the teary moments from *The Chosen*. I went directly to a good, old-fashioned dog movie to get in my feels.

I recognize most of you are probably a bit younger than me, but do you know the scene in *Air Bud* I'm talking about? If not, you might need to do a quick online search, but I'll warn you now, it's so, so sad! I'm pretty sure I first watched this movie when I was seven years old and the sadness still stings.

"You have to go, Buddy. Please, Buddy. Go! GET! GO!"[1] *Cue the sobs*

I quickly searched, "happy ending of Air Bud" to get myself out of this sad spell and write the rest of this chapter. I think my undealt with dog trauma needs to be addressed another time.

On a scale from 1-10, how comfortable are you with being sad?

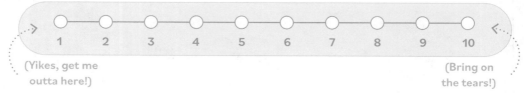

| 1 | 2 | 3 | 4 | 5 | 6 | 7 | 8 | 9 | 10 |

(Yikes, get me outta here!)   (Bring on the tears!)

Some of us are probably more familiar with sadness than others, but not one of us is immune to the heaviness, ache, and pain of this emotion. Sadness is the feeling you experience through heartbreak. When you have to look your best friend in the eyes and say that awful word, goodbye, not knowing when you'll talk to them again.

It's the feeling you experience through disappointment. When you worked really hard for something and it just didn't play out the way you hoped it would. It's the aftermath of a closed door.

Sadness is the feeling you experience through loss. Having to let go of someone you loved or a season you have to leave behind.

What have been the three greatest losses in your life?

I think a lot of us resonate more with the latter and have "sucked it up." We've convinced ourselves that our sadness is a burden to everyone around us. That if we're sad, we're going to kill the vibe, and eventually, no one's going to want to hang out with us. We're afraid of the reputation of becoming the "Debbie Downer" or "Negative Nancy" of our friend group, so we just move right along laughing, making sarcastic jokes, and joining the party. As you can imagine, that mentality doesn't sustain us for long.

Have you ever been there before? When was the last moment you remember feeling like you couldn't let yourself be sad?

The truth is, we've got to get a lot more comfortable having a tough day, being devastated over something, mourning losses, and grieving our past. It's a part of being human, and even more, there is beauty in our sadness. It gives us the gift of valuing and honoring life. When we experience sadness, it means that we cared and loved deeply. It's for the people who experienced life to the fullest!

There's this moment in Scripture that's a beautiful representation of honest sadness. It's the moment in John 20 after the death of Jesus, and Mary Magdalene was headed to the empty tomb.

First things first, let's back up a bit and look at the relationship between Mary and Jesus. They spent a lot of time together, and she's probably considered one of the most prominent women remembered from the life of Jesus. We are first introduced to her in Luke 8.

Stop and read Luke 8:1-2.

What does this Scripture tell us about Mary before meeting Jesus?

Before meeting Jesus, Mary was full of "evil spirits and sickness." As you can imagine, her life was dark and hopeless. Then she met Jesus, and through her faith, He saved her.

He literally brought her from death to life.

From that moment forward, she spent all her days following Jesus, learning from Him, witnessing miracle after miracle, supporting Him with her possessions (Luke 8:3), and standing beside Him when others rejected Him. Even when Jesus was taken to be crucified, Mary was there.

Standing by the cross of Jesus were his mother, his mother's sister, Mary the wife of Clopas, and Mary Magdalene.
JOHN 19:25

Even though it was a gruesome, terrible, and an incredibly sad moment to witness, Mary never missed an opportunity to honor and value her Savior. There would be no questions about Mary's love for Jesus.

Now let's get back in our Bibles and lean in a little closer to look at the moment Mary discovered that Jesus had risen.

Stop and read John 20:1-10.

It had been three long days of silence. The last memory she had was Jesus, her beloved teacher, being crucified right in front of her. She could probably still picture the blood dripping down Jesus's side, the look on His face as He hung there in agony, and the sound of His voice when He cried out His final words, "It is finished" (John 19:30).

Can you imagine the weight of sadness she must've experienced throughout those days? Reflect on this for a moment and write down what comes to mind.

When she arrived at the tomb, she saw that the stone sealing the entrance was not there. Immediately, she turned to go and tell her friends that something was off. In verses 3-4, we see Peter and John low-key competing to see who could get to the tomb first. When they arrived, they found the tomb empty just like Mary said it was. Peter and John decided to head back to Jerusalem, but Mary stayed put at the tomb.

Stop and read John 20:11-18.

What does Scripture say Mary did (v. 11)?

She sat there in the very raw feelings, in her sadness, and cried.

Have you ever been there before? Have you ever experienced such grief that you couldn't get off the floor or out of bed? Have you ever felt like you just didn't want to open your eyes to face reality again?

Using the space below, describe a time when you've experienced that kind of sadness and grief.

That's where Mary was at this moment. We can't know for sure the thoughts that ran through her mind. Maybe she thought Jesus's body had been stolen, maybe she thought someone was playing a cruel joke on her, or maybe the weight of her emotions from the days before finally caught up with her and she didn't even have the strength to get up and go from this place.

What does verse 16 tell us?

Jesus showed up. In the midst of her sorrow and sadness, He was there. The disciples, Peter and John, missed out on this one-on-one, face-to-face, intimate moment with Jesus. Mary got to be the first because she wasn't ashamed of her sadness. She sat there crying and didn't care if the whole world knew it.

Do you feel shame when you're sad? Why or why not?

In the same way as Mary, our sadness leads us to intimate encounters with Jesus. We have to stop being so afraid of this emotion, or we will miss out on what God has for us.

Sadness isn't something to run away from; it's not something to dismiss or be ashamed of. It's a beautiful, God-given feeling that invites us to know Him so much more.

THE SOUR SIDE: SELF-PITY

Kenz

Have you ever said the words, "It's no big deal. I'll just get over it"?

Literally lol'ing because I cannot tell you how many times I've said this. Pretty much anytime I'm really sad or disappointed in myself, these words come out of my mouth. It's my go-to. I'm scary good at convincing people of it at this point in my life. My mom, my sister, my closest friends would even tell you I'm tough, self-sufficient, and fine.

The most raw moment I can remember living this out was after a terrible breakup. Yep, you know we couldn't make it through a study about sadness without a good break up story. Well, here's a doozy of one!

I dated a guy for a really long time—five years to be exact. That was all through college and the first couple years after, and it's right about the time when it feels like eighty percent of your friends are getting engaged. That's right when we broke up. And let me tell you. It was rough!

Hands down, the hardest few months of my life, but no one knew that. I told people "I'm fine, and I'll get over it" about a thousand times, but inside I was falling apart.

When the sun went down and I was home alone, I wasn't fine at all. I was incredibly sad and heart broken. The thought of never speaking to my best friend again, never hugging him, holding hands, and never being together again was the worst thing ever. I spent my nights scrolling through my phone looking at photos of us and re-reading old text conversations. But no one knew that.

Everyone thought I was fine.

Soon enough my "I'm fine" mentality turned into the very sour side of sadness: *self-pity*. Externally, I celebrated my friends when they went on a good date or tied the knot, but internally, I was angry. I was constantly criticizing everyone's relationships and finding things that were annoying. It was all just to make myself feel better.

I felt like God had messed up my love story and I quietly hated Him for it.

I had so many questions, and He didn't give me any answers. It killed my confidence, instilled apathy, and swallowed me in a whole lot of self-doubt.

Have you ever been stuck in a place of self-pity like me? Maybe a bad breakup or something else drove you to self-pity. Get honest about that time in the space below.

There's a woman in Scripture who is honestly just so relatable when it comes to self-pity. Her name is Naomi and we're going to read about her story in the book of Ruth.

Let's dive in straight at the top!

Stop and read Ruth 1:1-5

What does this tell you about Naomi?

Verses 3-5 tell you that her husband and two sons had died. She lost everyone! Can you imagine the sadness and the weight of this? I feel like verse 6 should say, "She cried every day, and she was so sad." But, no, Naomi seemed to have the "I'm fine" mentality.

As we continue to read, I think it's important to remember to bring some creative imagination into reading Scripture. Let's practice this together. As you read, try to picture what Naomi looks like, what her hair texture was like, what her hands looked like, what she was wearing—all of the things!

Stop and read Ruth 1:6-22.

Write down your personal description of Naomi in the space below.

Here's my idea of Naomi. Scripture tells us that she had two sons who were newly married, so I'm guessing she's a middle-aged mother in her fifties. Knowing Naomi's toughness, I can imagine she looked about fifty too. I'm sure she endured the heat of the sun and had tough, leathery skin and deep beauty wrinkles to prove it. Her name stood for "pleasantness," and that seemed true of her as she was greatly loved by her family.[2] So much so that even her daughter-in-law wanted to spend the rest of her life with her. Everyone loved Naomi and loved her dearly.

What happened in verses 6-7?

The Lord provided food for his people in Judah, so Naomi wanted to go back and take part in it. Look below at verse 1, so you'll have a better understanding of this.

> *During the time of the judges, there was a famine in the land. A man left Bethlehem in Judah with his wife and two sons to stay in the territory of Moab for a while.*
> RUTH 1:1

Naomi and her family used to live in Bethlehem where God's people lived. However, because of a famine, Naomi's husband suggested that they move to the land of Moab. The bad thing was that the Moabites worshiped other gods and were not the best of people.

Naomi found herself in the land of Moab, but she was very much ready to go back to Bethlehem. Not only had the Lord again provided food back in Bethlehem, but this was also her true home, where her people were.

As she began to say goodbye to her daughters-in-law, we can somewhat see the sour side of her sadness beginning to surface. She's having to let go of the women she loved so dearly. Not only is she saying goodbye, but she has nothing and no one to go back to in Bethlehem. She's a widow now, and during that time, widows were looked down upon.

Life ahead was going to be hard for Naomi.

Fill in the blanks for Ruth 1:13-14

> "Would you be willing to wait for them to grow up? Would you restrain yourselves from remarrying? No, my daughters, my life is much too _____ for you to share, because the LORD's hand has turned against me." Again they _____ loudly, and Orpah kissed her mother-in-law, but Ruth clung to her."

Her daughters-in-law were weeping, but Naomi seemed as tough as bricks. She covered her tears with self-pity, blaming God, and not expecting how tough her feelings truly were.

Stop and read Ruth 1:19-22.

After a few long days of journeying through the wilderness, they finally made it to the edge of the village. Bethlehem was a super small village, so it was no surprise that the women recognized her as she made this tough walk back into town.

As soon as the women noticed her, she said:

> *"Don't call me Naomi. Call me Mara," she answered, "for the Almighty has made me very bitter. I went away full, but the Lord has brought me back empty. Why do you call me Naomi, since the Lord has opposed me, and the Almighty has afflicted me?"*
> RUTH 1:20-21

Anyone surprised by her self-proclaimed new name? Naomi wanted to change her name from "pleasantness" to "bitterness" because God had brought misfortune upon her.[3] In her shame and embarrassment, Naomi became hard-hearted and angry. She took on the "I'm fine" mentality, barely looking people in the eyes, avoiding her honest feelings, and casting blame on God. You can hear and see it all over the text.

But how do you think she was really feeling? Share your thoughts below.

Below the surface of that leathery skin and all those beauty wrinkles was a saddened heart. Naomi had just lost her husband, her two sons, and probably a lot of friends. Her heart was broken. She was sad and hopeless.

You see, she could have walked into the village and just cried. She could have let those tears flow and allowed herself to be held in her friend's arms. She could have admitted that she was hurting and lonely. She could have owned up to her grief and been met with forgiveness.

But in fear of being rejected, Naomi embodied self-pity. She was absorbed by her hardship and swallowed her sadness.

As we close out today and prepare for tomorrow's study on God's invitation in our sadness, I want you to finish reading Ruth 1–2 and see how Naomi began to come face-to-face with her grief, acknowledge her pain, and move through it with God. Not only that, but take note of how the Lord began to restore her joy.

Take notes as you read here: _____

_____

_____

_____

_____

_____

DAY 3

THE INVITATION: EMBRACE
Mac

Back in my brace-faced, queen of youth group, awkward middle school days, we used to play Bible verse memory games during Sunday school. We would go around a circle reciting as many verses by memory as we could recall. It never failed that the first person to go always started with John 11:35—the shortest verse in the Bible.

"Jesus wept."

In middle school, it was an easy answer to guarantee a free candy bar, but as I've gotten older, it's a verse that stops me in my tracks. Two words that carry such a deeper story. John 11:35 proves that our Jesus knew what it was like to mourn and feel the weight of sadness. He allowed Himself to be so filled with emotion from the loss of a friend that He was moved to literal tears. Jesus, fully God, King of kings, and Savior of the world wasn't immune to the human experience of loss and grief.

Today we're going to take a deeper look at this profound story from John 11 to see the invitation that Jesus offers all of us when we feel burdened by the heavy weight of sadness.

Stop and read John 11:1-16.

Who do we find out is sick in verse 1?

Lazarus and his sisters, Mary and Martha, were close friends of Jesus. You can read more about their interactions in Luke 10:38-42. It seemed that Jesus had visited their home before and developed a personal relationship with them. So, when Lazarus fell ill, Mary and Martha sent word to Jesus.

What does Jesus do when he finds out about Lazarus (vv. 5-6)?

He stayed put for two whole days. Okay, hold up! What are you doing, Jesus?

I don't know about you, but even when I'm simply in a wardrobe crisis and I call a friend for help, I expect them to drop everything at a moment's notice to come to my rescue. But Jesus, in an actual crisis, did the opposite!

I want you to picture this moment in your mind: Mary and Martha watching as their brother's health slowly declines, gradually growing weaker, the life draining from his once joy-filled face. They know that Jesus has the incredible power to heal, so in their most desperate moment, they send word to Him that Lazarus is ill. I can picture them quietly glancing at the door every few minutes, anxiously awaiting the arrival of the only One who could change the outcome of their situation.

But He didn't show.

Lazarus died and it seemed like all hope was lost.

Can you imagine how devastated Mary and Martha must have felt? They had a deeply personal relationship with this man who healed strangers, turned water into wine, made a feast out of a mere snack, and for some reason, He didn't show up for them. I wonder if like we talked about yesterday, their sadness had turned sour and the lies of self-pity had begun to infiltrate their minds.

Have you ever had a moment when you felt like Jesus didn't show up for you? Describe it here. How did you feel?

Isn't it true that Jesus always has a way of doing things His own way? With Mary and Martha, Jesus waited when they wanted Him to go, and with the disciples, He went when they wanted Him to wait (v. 8). I know from my own life experience that God doesn't play games with me. He's a God of clarity and peace, but if I'm being honest, His timing often frustrates me.

I have to actively remind myself that His ways are not our ways, and His timing is not always our timing. The path of Jesus doesn't always make sense in our rational brains, but His plan is always so much greater than anything we can rationally fathom. That's why when we feel the confusion and disarray that often comes with sadness, we have to train our hearts to go to Jesus.

Upon Jesus's arrival in Bethany, He was met individually by both of the sisters. First, Jesus spoke with Martha and comforted her by telling her that her brother would rise again. Then He spoke with Mary.

Stop and read John 11:17-37.

When Jesus saw Mary, His friend whom He loved, and heard the pain in her voice, it evoked something in Him emotionally. The Scripture tells us that Jesus was "deeply moved in his Spirit and troubled" (v. 33). One look and Jesus could probably see that her heart was breaking in two.

Despite fully knowing the eventual outcome of this situation (spoiler alert: Lazarus would rise again), Jesus paused and responded compassionately, fully allowing Himself to feel the weight of that moment. As Mary wept for her brother, Jesus, the Son of God began to weep too.

Try to imagine Jesus in this moment. What do you think His posture was? What did His face look like? How do you think the people around Him responded?

I think when we're feeling sad, we're often quick to try and run from it. We feel ashamed of our tears. No joke—every time I cry around anyone, the first thing that comes out of my mouth is "I'm sorry!"

Which choice below best describes your relationship with crying?

| What? I never cry! | I'm pretty amazing at hiding my tears. | I cry only with people I'm comfortable with. | I cry fairly often. | I cry all day, every day! |

For some reason, myself and probably many of you reading this have been cultured to believe that our tears of sadness are a sign of weakness that we should be embarrassed of, that we shouldn't bother other people with, and that we should quietly wipe them away and keep moving.

But how profound is it that Jesus allowed Himself to surrender to and beautifully dwell in a moment of sadness? I mean, think about it! He knew that Lazarus's resurrection was on the horizon, but rather than skipping straight to it, He fully embraced the beauty and importance of what it means to grieve for the loss of something of value.

When we're swimming deep in our own grief, I believe that Jesus is offering us all the beautiful invitation of embrace. He calls us to first embrace Him—to run to Him, to fall at His feet, and to cast our worries, cares, and tears right there.

Then I think He invites us to embrace what we're feeling with Him. Sadness isn't something to be ashamed of; it's the emotion that speaks to how deeply we value something in our lives—someone we love or something we've lost. The more we value something or someone, the more sadness we will feel when it's gone.

You see, when you're feeling sad, Jesus isn't telling you to "suck it up, buttercup." No, just like His response to Mary's grief, He responds with compassion. He feels what you feel, gets in it with you, and embraces you as you grieve and honor what you lost.

+ That crushing breakup, Jesus is inviting you to grieve it with Him.
+ That feeling of deeply missing home, feel it at the feet of Jesus.
+ The sadness you feel from the loss of a friendship, Jesus is in it with you.
+ The tears you cried over the death of a dream, mourn it with Jesus.

So many of us have trained our hearts to run from sadness, but in effect, we have numbed our hearts to everything else. John 11 shows us that Jesus embraced sadness because He knew that it was a gift that allows the heart to do what it is ultimately created to do—love deeply.

Is there any sadness in your life that you've been fighting against or refusing to feel? How does it point to something that you loved and cared for deeply?

Jesus is inviting you to grieve, mourn, and cry as a sign of honor, recognition, and value for the things that truly matter. People, relationships, hopes, dreams, and friendships are all gifts from God that we are invited to love deeply when we have them and mourn deeply when we lose them. Scripture shows us that sadness is God's design for us to cleanse our hearts by running to Him when the world fails us. That's the gift of feeling the fullness of your sadness and letting it lead you to His loving embrace.

I love that in verse 36, in response to Jesus's tears, the Jews gathered there that day said this: "See how he loved him!"

Tears of sadness are a signpost for what we love. That's not something to be ashamed of, that's something to embrace! Rather than running away from our feelings of grief, Jesus invites us to embrace Him as we embrace the pain of grieving the things that truly matter.

Picture Jesus with you at this moment. What do you think He would say about the thing you're currently grieving (big or small) in your life?

LIVE IN EMBRACE
Mac

About a year ago, I moved into a new home. It was my first time not living in a dorm room, a shared apartment, or a house that belonged to my parents. For the first time I was going to have a space that I could completely call my own. I remember thinking that I wanted it to be a space that felt like "home" for as many people as possible.

A couple of days before moving in, my mom and I went over to the house to roll out the rugs to give them enough time to flatten before moving in my furniture. After completing our task, we sat in my empty house on the newly unrolled rugs and prayed for the conversations that would take place in that space in the years to come.

We asked that God would make it a safe place, a place where as soon as women walked in the door, they'd feel as if they could be completely themselves. A place where they were free to let their walls down, to confess the things they'd never told anyone before, a space to simply feel so seen, loved, and accepted, and even somewhere you could shed a few tears if you needed to.

Three months later, after forgetting about that prayer, I assembled a hodgepodge group of about ten women on a random Wednesday night for a new Bible study. For our first time together, I asked everyone to go around the circle and share where they were at with the Lord and what they were hoping to get out of our time together. No exaggeration here—as each girl shared, tears poured out of their eyes as they spoke of heartbreak, loss, disappointment, confusion, and really tough seasons that they were in the midst of. I think we legitimately went through an entire box of tissues just on the first night!

As I sat and listened, sitting on the rug that my mom and I had rolled out just months before, I remembered our prayers. God had answered in the most beautiful way! Romans 12:15 popped into my head at that moment.

> *"Rejoice with those who rejoice; weep with those who weep."*
> ROMANS 12:15

We were right in the middle of God's design for us—celebrating and rejoicing, while also mourning and weeping together! Sadness was never meant to be kept hidden away in the depths of our hearts, but rather shared with one another.

Carrying each other's burdens and allowing others to carry ours is what Jesus has called us to. It's a beautiful picture of the gospel in action that I got to witness in the warm glow of my living room light.

Although nobody technically walked away "fixed" that night—because we all had the same problems and situations awaiting us when our time ended—we all truly felt a common bond to one another that carried us through the next eight weeks together. And more importantly, that moment made us all realize how embraced we were by the loving arms of a Father who saw our struggles and came running to us.

This week, as you meet as a group to talk through the invitation Jesus offers you in the midst of feeling sad, don't be afraid to get raw, cry if you have to, reach into the dark corners of your heart, and unpack the things you've quietly tucked away. I have no doubt that there are women on either side of you who are more than ready to embrace you and walk with you and all your mascara-stained-cheeks glory straight to the feet of Jesus.

OPEN IT UP:

1. **Which of the eight core feelings are you most feeling at this moment?**

2. **Think back on your childhood. What's your earliest memory of sadness?**

LET'S GET REAL:

1. What sadness are you experiencing in your life right now? Where does it stem from? What does it feel like?

2. Have you been numbing, avoiding, or running away from your sadness? Why have you been doing this? How have you seen it turn into self pity?

LIVING INTO THE INVITATION:

When you're feeling sad, Jesus isn't telling you to get over it and move on. He responds with compassion just as He did in Mary's grief. He feels what you feel, gets in it with you, and embraces you as you grieve.

1. Have you been going to Jesus in your grief? Who or what have you gone to instead?

2. What could it look like for you to embrace the Lord in your sadness? How do you sense Him embracing you?

GIVING THE INVITATION:

Just as Jesus showed up for Mary and Martha in their grief, we can show up for our friends and family and help to embrace them as they walk through their sadness.

1. Write down the name of someone in your life who is currently walking through a season of deep sadness.

2. How might Jesus be calling you to embrace them in this season? What would it look like for you to step into their grief?

WHEN I'M FEELING ANGRY

WEEK 4

LISTEN

As we begin this next week, scan the QR code to join us for a conversation all about anger. In this podcast episode, we talk about how we've both personally experienced and felt anger in the past, plus how we're learning to bring it to the feet of Jesus to allow us to respond in love.

THE CORE FEELING: ANGER

Mac

What if I told you that angry people live the most abundant lives?

My guess would be that you'd argue with me (maybe angrily) and tell me all the reasons that I'm crazy and wrong for thinking that anger adds any value to people's lives. In some ways, you would make a valid argument. Anger has certainly led to a lot of destruction, hurt, and pain in our world. It's often the root of some of the most hurtful words we've ever dared to utter. It's the springboard for some of our worst decisions, and perhaps the initial cause of our deepest pain.

Think back on a time you felt intensely angry. What did it lead you to do?

In our anger, many of us have written off and excluded some of the people we loved the most from our lives. (Cough, cough, cancel culture.)

We've harshly said or done hurtful things we didn't mean to people who didn't deserve it.

We've raged on the internet when someone posted something we disagreed with.

We've angrily given our friends the silent treatment when they've wronged us.

We've allowed our anger to trap us in arguments, and we can't even remember the reason we got into them in the first place.

Anger has a funny way of turning us into a version of ourselves that we don't like. But what if anger in itself isn't the problem? What if it's simply the way we've been taught to process or push aside our anger?

On a scale from 1-10, how comfortable are you currently with feeling anger?

1 2 3 4 5 6 7 8 9 10

This week, we're going to look to God's Word to explore some of the misconceptions we all have when it comes to anger, and then dig into it's important connection to our spiritual lives.

One of the most prominent stories from the Bible that we often connect anger to is Jesus flipping the tables in the temple. This story shows up four different times in the Gospels. It seemed to happen once during the early days of Jesus's ministry as described in John 2 and then again towards the end of His life as described in the synoptic Gospels (Matthew, Mark, and Luke). Let's read one of the accounts together.

Stop and read John 2:13-17.

How did Jesus respond when He witnessed what was happening in the temple?

The writer John tells us that after Jesus arrived in Jerusalem for Passover and entered the temple gates, He saw a scene that deeply affected Him emotionally. He fashioned a whip and began to drive out the money changers, poured out their money, and even started flipping tables.

Now maybe Jesus flipped those tables tenderly, slowly, and graciously, but my guess is that He did it with a bit more flare, spice, and authority. Jesus wasn't messing around! Now maybe you're thinking, *like woahhhhh, Jesus! Why are you going all* Real Housewives of New Jersey *up in the temple? Aren't you supposed to be a bit more calm in these situations?*

What comes to mind when you think about Jesus getting angry in this way?

I get it! This moment seems to be a bit out of character for Jesus. But think about this, have you ever been angry about an injustice in the world? Does child abuse or human trafficking have a rightful response on you emotionally? Jesus was witnessing firsthand an injustice and He wasn't going to let it go.

The temple was a sacred place meant for worship and for God to connect with His people. From all over the world, people would travel to Jerusalem for Passover to worship in the temple. In order to do this, they would need to exchange their money for temple coins so they could purchase an animal to sacrifice.[1] According to Jesus, these merchants were a "den of thieves" (Matt. 21:13) who were more than likely charging outrageous rates and taking advantage of those who had no other options.

Not to mention that these sellers had also set up shop in the Court of the Gentiles, which was the furthest place Gentiles were allowed in the temple at that time to worship and connect with God.[2] This crowded the temple and interrupted the atmosphere of worship. It more than likely even prevented certain people from getting in.

As the sellers were making dishonest gains and interrupting the atmosphere of worship, Jesus experienced true anger at the injustice of this moment. But His anger reveal the truth of His heart—His deep respect and honor for His Father's house. At this very moment, the disciples reflected on a Scripture passage from the psalms that prophesied and connected to this moment.

Turn to Psalm 69:9 and fill in the blanks:

Because _____ for your house has _____ me, and the insults of those who insult you have fallen on me.

It was Jesus's zeal or passion for His Father's house that was underneath His anger in the temple courts. Let's pause and process how powerful this is together.

How does knowing Jesus's heart and passion change your view of His anger in this moment?

Many of us have been taught to believe that anger is a negative emotion that we should immediately cut out of our lives. When we experience anger, we feel as if we've more than likely fallen short, not shown enough patience, or let others get to us. But what if anger is actually a gift that we can use to ultimately reveal or unlock the contents of our hearts? What if anger actually uncovers our true passions? What if it's a tool that can be used for the benefit of all relationships?

Jesus, the man who never sinned, felt the fullness of anger and even acted upon it. His anger revealed to the people around Him a zeal, love, and commitment to the holiness of His Father's house and the protection of the sacred worship between God and His people. His anger compelled Him to action to defend and protect something He deeply valued.

The truth is that anger is one of the most vulnerable emotions that we can feel because it reveals and clarifies what our hearts have been quietly yearning for and what we ultimately care about. When we feel angry, we often can't hide the other emotions that we've been suppressing or avoiding. Everything bubbles to the surface and the truth always comes out. There's always a deeper story underneath feelings of anger.

Although anger isn't always steeped in ultimate reason or truth, it's incredibly beautiful and helpful as it reveals the authentic truth of who we are. You just can't hide when you feel angry. Anger is a check engine light for our hearts. It tells us and everyone around us that something is wrong and desperately needs to be tended to.

What is something you're currently angry about or experiencing anger in?

How does your anger typically express itself? (Do you let it freely fly with your words or your actions? Do you suppress it? Does it seep out through passive-aggressive actions?)

When we experience anger, we are quick to want to find somewhere or someone to place the blame. Culture tells us that we should simply cancel people who don't agree with our political views, cut out all the "toxic" people from our lives, and create better boundaries so people can't ever get to us. But that's so far from what Jesus was about! Jesus didn't shy away from the people who made Him angry, He leaned in from a place of love.

Anger is not an excuse to sin, hate, abandon, or cancel. Instead, it is the God-given feeling that should move us toward love. Anger as created by God was never designed to be tossed aside. Rather, it should lead us back to the feet of Jesus to be processed through His gaze and His heart. It's with Him that we can lean into anger to understand the deeper story it's telling, then allow Him to help us respond in love.

This week, we're going to explore together how we can use biblical anger to live a more abundant life. It's a life that allows our hearts to be seen, understood, and compelled to respond with loving action.

THE SOUR SIDE: BITTERNESS
Mac

We couldn't write a Bible study on anger without addressing the hard fact that many of us have been deeply affected and forever changed by someone else's anger. My guess would be that all of us at one point or another have been the recipient of hate-filled words, angry rants, or aggressive actions.

Share two or three experiences in your life when you have been the recipient of anger.

How hurt did those situations leave you feeling on a scale from 1-10?

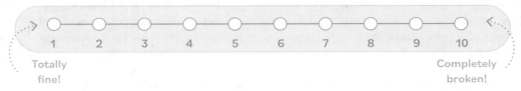

1	2	3	4	5	6	7	8	9	10

Totally fine!   Completely broken!

The hard truth is that anger, maybe more than any of the other seven core feelings, has the very real possibility of turning extremely sour. While biblical anger compels us into deeper love, the anger we often experience in our world today can quickly morph into hate, hurt, and abuse. This is why it's so important to learn how to process with God through the very natural emotion of anger.

Today we're going to dive into the story of a very angry, bitter, and unhappy person from Scripture. His name is Jonah. You have probably heard about this prophet that got eaten by a fish, tossed into the ocean, and still had to go to the very people he hated to proclaim God's message for them. Many of us have a Sunday school version of Jonah's story, but I want to look at it today with fresh eyes and from the lens of what can happen when we allow our anger to turn sour.

Stop and read Jonah 1.

Okay, wow! A lot just went down in seventeen verses. Let's recap this all together.

Fill in the blanks below:

The Lord told Jonah to go to _____ to preach against it because of its evil and wickedness (v. 1).

Jonah was like nahhhhhh man! He decided to flee to_____ (v. 2).

Jonah boarded a boat in Joppa to try and run away, so the Lord sent a huge_____ (v. 4).

Jonah was _____ while the crew was rightfully flipping out (v. 5). They tossed him overboard and the storm finally stopped.

Jonah was swallowed by a_____. He was in its belly for _____ days (v. 17).

This is one wild theatrical performance, and honestly, it only gets crazier! In Jonah 2, we see Jonah call out to the Lord from the fish's belly and ask for deliverance. The Lord hears Jonah's prayers, speaks to the fish (crazy!), and it vomits Jonah out on dry land. Okay, ew!

In Jonah 3, we finally see Jonah respond in obedience to God's original call. He goes to the city of Nineveh and delivers the message God had entrusted with him. And guess what? The people believed in God, repented, fasted, and then stopped their evil actions and violence. Even the king repented and bowed down to God! God sees their change of heart, responds in mercy, and stops His plan to destroy them.

WOO-HOO! This is a cause for celebration, right? Well, not quite for everyone.

Stop and read Jonah 4.

How does Jonah feel about God's decision to show mercy to the Ninevites (v. 1)?

He's angry! Despite the fact that his preaching worked, the Ninevites repented, and his mission was complete, Jonah was seething with anger and bitterness. In his mind, the Ninevites were the worst of the worst, and they didn't deserve God's love and mercy. I don't know about you, but this feels almost slightly uncomfortable to read. It's totally cringe-worthy! Like why was Jonah being such a baby? Couldn't he just get over it?

I want to judge Jonah, but if I get super honest, this has been the posture of my own heart more often than I'd like to admit. There have been plenty of times when my anger has led me to pridefully believe that I deserve more of something than someone else, that I know more than they do, or that I'm simply all-around better than them.

When we don't process our anger at the feet of Jesus, when we try to push it aside, or when we respond irrationally to it, something inside of us turns sour and morphs into bitterness. It is similar to resentment, the sour side of hurt, but with anger attached to it, bitterness can often become more hostile and harsh.

Recently, my best friend from college got engaged. We went to dinner a few weeks after her engagement, and during dessert, she asked me to be a bridesmaid in her wedding. I was ecstatic to stand beside her on her big day! After we celebrated, she began telling me about all the other girls she was asking to be bridesmaids too. I smiled and nodded along listening to the entire list until she got to the last name.

Helloooo, bitterness!

Just in the months prior, I had walked through a tough season of friendship with this mutual friend of ours. And honestly, it had left me feeling angry and upset with her. But had I processed those feelings? Nope! I had pushed them aside and tried to pretend like I wasn't upset. For the most part, it had worked, up until that moment.

Sitting across the table from my friend, panic and ugly bitterness began to stew in my heart. I started mentally making a list of all the reasons why she shouldn't ask her, why I was a better friend, and why I deserved to be a bridesmaid more than her.

I cringe thinking back on this because it's so far from the way I wish I would've responded in that moment. I wonder how I would've reacted if I had just allowed my anger to lead me towards admitting my hurt and fighting for reconciliation, rather than tossing it aside and letting it quietly eat away at my heart.

How have you seen bitterness slip into a relationship when you've avoided feelings of anger?

The truth is bitterness lies about feeling hurt. It cannot admit fault. It doesn't seek forgiveness, and it makes excuses for hurtful behavior. It justifies instead of reconciles, and it blocks the truth of the harm that it inevitably causes.

While anger invites us to vulnerably admit the truth of our hearts and respond in love, bitterness entices us to react with hate. Jonah fell victim to this. And I fall victim to this all the time, and I'm guessing that maybe you do too.

What harm have you seen your own bitterness cause? What lies has it convinced you to believe?

Here's what is so scary and alarming about this: if we don't deal with our bitterness, it can lead us to dangerous and impaired versions of anger.

One of the byproducts of undealt bitterness is an impaired version of anger called defeat or depression.[3] This is the total refusal to feel any anger at all. It's a coping mechanism that many of us use to control, avoid, or push aside the exposing vulnerability of our anger. We'd rather feel nothing than have to come face to face with our other undealt emotions. We see this expressed in the way that Jonah's story ends.

Stop and read Jonah 4:8-9.

After Jonah's angry rant to God, he went and sat outside Nineveh where God had provided a shady place for him to rest under a tree while awaiting the fate of the city. In the morning, God sent a worm to eat the tree and totally destroyed Jonah's place of comfort. Jonah couldn't hide any longer and he admitted total defeat telling God, "I'm angry enough to die" (v. 9).

Jonah had let his anger turn into unhealthy bitterness that led him to a place of defeat. He seriously started to believe that death was better than life, that numbing out was better than feeling, that being isolated was better than loving his enemies. He had let bitterness eat away at his heart and steal the joy of living from him.

So many of us are eerily close to walking down this same path. We've let our bitterness build a hundred-foot wall around our hearts, and we're convinced that simply giving up, walking away, or numbing out is the only way to stop the pain and hurt of life. This is an evil plot of the enemy!

Is there any impaired anger in your life that has been thwarted into defeat or depression? Confess it here.

Jonah's story is a warning sign to us all about what happens when we let our anger turn sour rather than bringing it to God. Tomorrow, we will dive into the invitation that Jesus offers us when we feel angry. Because with Him, there is a beautiful and powerful restoration that awaits us on the other side of our anger.

THE INVITATION: PASSION

Kenz

I'll be honest in saying that until recently, I never thought there could be a positive spin on anger.

As most of you know by now, Mac and I are best friends, business partners, and practically sisters at this point. And well, Mac is the "passionate one." Throughout the years we've had to make some really big decisions together, and it sparked some seriously heated conversations.

I'll tell you how it usually goes: It's a casual Tuesday and we'll be mid-conversation about a decision that needs to be made in the next couple weeks. Something suddenly ignites her moral compass and we quickly find ourselves in a full-on, blow-out of an argument. In these moments, it's easy for me to judge her, get critical, and rethink why in the world we've committed to this whole thing. But by the grace of God, we've stuck it out and have learned oh so much through the process.

As you know by now, anger is a tough feeling to navigate. It can turn sour really quickly, but there's a sweet side of it that I don't want any of us to miss.

The truth is, if Mac had ignored her anger over the years, we would have made a whole lot of silly decisions. It's her anger that has uprooted injustice, created better ideas, led to healing conversations, kept us on the right path, and been extremely vital in carrying out the ministry. I can honestly tell you that every heated conversation, heart-to-heart, or moment we had to dig in a little deeper has been one hundred percent worth it.

Take a moment to see the fruitful side of anger. How has your anger or someone else's anger uprooted injustice, created a healthy conversation, or produced good fruit in your life?

When we're angry, we have the invitation to lean into passion, to fight for something that we care deeply about, and to stand firm in what we believe in. Think about Martin Luther King, Jr., Mother Teresa, Abraham Lincoln—these people are marked by passion. But before we get much further, let's look at Jesus.

It's not hard to pick up on the fact that Jesus is pretty heated in this passage of Scripture. For the last couple of days, He had been traveling, teaching, and healing; meanwhile, everyone was trying to gang up on Him.

What does Scripture say in verse 2?

The onlookers and other teachers of the law were trying to find reasons to accuse Him. I can imagine that people were lurking around Him and judging His every move. Annoying, right? I'd be angry all the time and not in a good way!

On this particular day, the day of Sabbath, He walked into the synagogue and noticed a man with a shriveled hand. Jesus was well aware of the religious expectations of the Sabbath—you weren't allowed to work, do household chores, or heal on this day. But Jesus wasn't afraid to break religious norms for the sake of healing and salvation.

You can hear the authoritative passion in Jesus's voice as He says to the man, "Stand before us" (v. 3).

He had no intention of hiding this miracle or waiting until the crowds went away. He wanted to prove a point to the onlookers and exemplify the true heart of God to those watching.

How did the crowd respond when Jesus questioned them (v. 4)?

Scripture says that they were silent. They didn't care. Their hearts didn't break for this man like His did. They didn't share the same passion.

This sent Jesus into a tizzy. Okay, maybe not a tizzy, but He was angry! Not because they were annoying, lurking, and pestering Him, but because this was a perfect opportunity for His critics to change their minds about Him and their traditions. But their hearts were hardened, and they rejected Him completely.

But, like a boss, Jesus followed through with the miracle and the man's hand was healed.

Fill in the blank for Mark 3:5.

> After looking around at them with_____, he was grieved at the hardness of their hearts and told the man, "Stretch out your hand." So he stretched it out, and his hand was restored.

You see, the root of His anger was passion. His passion led to this man's healing. Regardless of what anyone thought, He cared about this man. He saw how he must have been tossed aside and ignored by the rest of the world.

He cared about the man and His anger compelled Him.

What has made you angry recently? How might your anger be attached to your passions? .

As we close out for today, I want to look at the final moments of Jesus's life on earth, the passion of the cross. Have you ever wondered why it's called the passion of the cross? It's not just a clever movie title or a Christian cliché—there's actually significance behind it.

Stop and read Luke 22:42-44.

Fill in the blank for Luke 22:44.

Being in _____, he prayed more fervently, and his sweat became like drops of blood falling to the ground.

Jesus walked on earth knowing that He was responsible for taking on the sins of the world. Every day He faced that reality. Yet people betrayed, lied, falsely accused, and ignored Him. Have you ever thought that this might have made Him angry?

Of course, it did!

Put yourself in Jesus's shoes: If you knew you were the Son of God and no one believed you, yet you were still planning on dying for their sins, how angry would you be on an everyday basis on a scale from 1-10?

| 1 | 2 | 3 | 4 | 5 | 6 | 7 | 8 | 9 | 10 |

(No biggie.)

(I'd change my mind about everything!)

Jesus's anger stirred the passion that led Him to the cross. He was willing to be in pain for something that mattered far more than the pain itself. Passion is the gift of anger. If you love something enough, you're willing to die for it.

That's the passion of the cross.

So the next time you're tempted to subdue or quiet your feelings of anger, maybe you need to lean into the underlying passion. Maybe there is something that God is trying to call you into. Maybe He's trying to stir something new inside of you. Maybe He's wanting to highlight someone to you. Maybe He's counting on you to take on the passion of the cross, like Jesus, and endure the pain for the sake of the gospel.

What might God be revealing about your passions through this week?

LIVE IN PASSION

Kenz

If you're anything like me, you were probably pretty shook by this week's study. So many of us have placed a negative connotation on our anger or the angry feelings of others, and it probably feels like quite the feat to rewrite this narrative. Not only that, but I cannot help but assume so many of you might be thinking about certain verses in Scripture that have always taught you that anger isn't a good thing. Verses such as:

> *Be angry and do not sin: Don't let the sun go down on your anger.*
> EPHESIANS 4:26

> *My dear brothers and sisters, understand this: Everyone should be quick to listen, slow to speak, and slow to anger.*
> JAMES 1:19-20

> *A hot-tempered person stirs up conflict, but one slow to anger calms strife.*
> PROVERBS 15:18

> *But now, put away all the following: anger, wrath, malice, slander, and filthy language from your mouth.*
> COLOSSIANS 3:8

> *Therefore, the LORD was very angry with Israel, and he removed them from his presence. Only the tribe of Judah remained.*
> 2 KINGS 17:18

Instead of sharing our perspective, we thought it might be fun for you to wrestle with some of these well known verses about anger with your group this week. As you prepare for the group, study a couple of these verses a little deeper, ask yourself the hard questions, and seek new understanding from God's Word.

What is Paul getting at when he says, "Don't let the sun go down on your anger" (Eph. 4:26)? Does he really think things are going to get better when I'm sleep deprived and cranky?

Is James telling us to be passive aggressive and not let our passions rise up in us or is he just giving us a better way to handle our anger (James 1:19-20)?

Can you be angry without being hot tempered? Can you be patient and angry at the same time? Is it bad to stir up conflict? How is David teaching us to be angry (Prov. 15:8)?

When does anger become a sin? What are tell-tale signs that our anger has turned sour (Col. 3:8)?

How have you seen God's anger in a negative light? Why do you think He was angry? How did His anger bring you freedom (2 Kings 17:18)?

OPEN IT UP:

1. Which of the eight core feelings are you most feeling at this moment?

Hurt   Lonely   Sad   Anger   Fear   Shame   Guilt   Joy

2. Since we're talking about anger this week, start off by sharing the thing that makes you the MOST mad. You don't need to get too serious yet, just something that first comes to mind.

LET'S GET REAL:

1. Is there a verse from the group intro that the Lord highlighted to you? How was it convicting? What new revelation did you receive?

2. What has stirred or surfaced anger in your life most recently? If you're being honest, has it turned into bitterness or has it been refining?

LIVING INTO THE INVITATION:

Chances are that a whole lot of you have been subduing anger inside of you for a while now, assuming that it's not okay to be angry. But maybe Jesus is inviting you to live a life full of passion. Maybe He's calling on you to uproot injustice, help others see things they cannot, and create fruitful conversations that are often easier to avoid.

1. What anger have you subdued in your life?

2. How do you feel God calling you to express this anger in a passionate, biblical way? When this anger is surfaced, how do you envision it impacting the world around you?

GIVING THE INVITATION:

Most of us have someone in our lives that we've cut off because of their hot temper or aggressive anger. Although it might not have been handled in the best way, chances are they are simply unaware of how to navigate their angry feelings and are possibly ashamed of the way they acted.

1. Who is the first person that comes to mind?

2. What do you think they ultimately care about underneath their angry actions or feelings?

3. What could it look like for you to have a healing conversation with them? How can your group keep you accountable to practically step out in that this week?

WHEN I'M FEELING AFRAID

WEEK 5

LISTEN

Scan the QR code to join us for a conversation all about fear. In this podcast episode, we talk about seasons where we've experienced fear, when our faith has felt weary, and how God has built our faith back up.

THE CORE FEELING: FEAR

Kenz

Fear comes in all different shapes and sizes.

It's the feeling you get looking down from thirty feet above the water while everyone's waiting for you to jump. Your heart starts beating faster, your palms are sweating, and your mind is racing with all possible outcomes.

It's the feeling you get sitting in the lobby of the emergency room waiting to hear the results of your dad's sudden illness. There's a knot in your stomach that makes you want to throw up. The silence around you is so heavy that you want to run away.

It's the feeling you get after an incredible first date. In the moment you were doing great, but the second you walk away, your self-confidence begins to tank. You replay every move in your head, cringing at the things you said and saying it'll be fine even when you don't actually believe it.

It's the feeling you get when you wake up to a sudden noise in the middle of the night. Your heart stops beating and you hold your breath in an attempt to hide yourself. You lie there for hours waiting for your nerves to calm back down to normal.

Describe the last time you can remember experiencing fear.

Fear has a way of controlling us. It builds walls in our hearts and removes our emotions to protect us from getting hurt. Fear takes away our trust of anyone or anything, and as a result, creates a self-sufficient and impulsive mentality. It tells us to control a life in which we will never be able to control, often sending us into a downward spiral of anxiety.

When have you let your fear control you? Why do you think you let it get to that point?

But like all of our feelings, fear offers an invitation into deeper intimacy with Jesus. When we admit our fear, we become strong—not in our own strength, but by the strength of the Lord.

Fear invites us into deeper dependency on God and to fully experience the comfort of His presence.

But before we get much further, let's take a look at someone in Scripture right in the middle of a moment of fear. We are going to open up our Bibles to Mathew 14 and read about this moment when Peter, one of the disciples, was brave enough to walk on water.

Stop and read Mathew 14:22-34.

Peter was known to be one of the more angsty, bold, and brave disciples. Most people actually knew him to be fearless, especially when it came to being in the water. He was a fisherman and had spent hundreds of days out there in some pretty gnarly storms. If they had surfed back then, he one hundred percent would've been the guy catching those tsunami like waves and swimming with the sharks.

On this particular day, there was a storm on the horizon and the water was already starting to get pretty rough. Jesus decided He was going to join the guys on the boat, but it had already gone pretty far out in the water. So instead of asking them to come get Him, Jesus walked to them on the water. Pretty casual, right?

What does verse 26 say?

They thought Jesus was a ghost and feared for their lives! I can imagine they all ducked behind the edge of the boat, piled on top of each other like sardines. "John, get off me, you're digging into my ribs. Thomas stop talking. James, shhhhhhh, I don't want to die!"

Fill in the blanks from Matthew 14:27.

Immediately Jesus spoke to them, "Have _____! It is I. Don't be _____."

I'm sure the disciples began whispering among themselves, "Really? Is that Jesus? I didn't know He could walk on water!"

Peter, not convinced of this yet, bravely stood up to find out for himself.

What did Peter say to Jesus? And how did Jesus respond to him?

I'm sure Peter was slightly taken back, "Oh snaps, it is You!" As soon as he heard this, he probably gave himself a little pump-up speech, shook off any nerves, and started to get out of the boat.

Have you ever experienced the "oh, I'm about to actually do this" kind of moment? What did this feel like?

I'm sure that as soon as Peter began to take his first step off the boat and onto the water, his heart started to beat a little faster. The first step confident and courageous, then immediately questioning if he was going to stay standing. By the next step, the realization of reality started to sink in. Peter began to panic a little and moved his eyes off Jesus and onto the giant waves that were surrounding him. And just like that, he started to sink.

This is the moment when Peter began to experience what we are talking about today—fear. The Greek word for fear is *phobeō*, which means "to flee" or "to put to flight."[1] When we are afraid, we emotionally flee, disconnecting ourselves from Jesus and trying to control the situation for ourselves. Our fear innately tells us to take control.

But here's the thing. Fear tells us to take control of things we never can ultimately control. As we all know, Peter couldn't walk on water on his own. It was only through the power of Jesus that he could do this miraculous thing.

As Peter began to sink, what did he yell out (v. 30)?

Rather than letting his fear turn into control, Peter asks Jesus for help. A simple cry that changed everything!

Scripture says that Jesus immediately reached out His hand and caught Peter. Rather than getting so caught up in his own pride, self-defense, and pretending he could do it on his own, Peter asked Jesus to show up and that's exactly what He did.

Did you know that it's the same for us? When we find ourselves in our most desperate moment, all we have to do is call upon the name of Jesus, and He will show up.

Some of you might have given up on Jesus showing up for a while now. Maybe it's been so long since you have invited Him into your fear that you've convinced yourself He doesn't even care anymore. That if you ask Him for help, He's just going to ignore you.

Some of you might have begun believing that your fear is too big for Him. That at this point in your life, it's almost easier to manage it on your own. You've become self-sufficient and hard-hearted. It's not that you want it this way, but you cannot see it being any other way.

Some of you have begun believing that Scripture is just some nut case's story from when Jesus walked on earth and it's not applicable to your fears today. You don't believe that Jesus has the power to walk on water, and He definitely doesn't have the power to help you with your fear.

Describe how you've been dealing with your fear recently. Explain why you have or have not turned to Jesus for help.

On a scale from 1-10, where is your faith? Do you believe that Jesus really will show up for you?

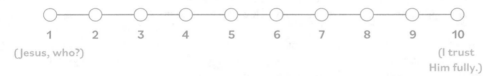

| 1 | 2 | 3 | 4 | 5 | 6 | 7 | 8 | 9 | 10 |

(Jesus, who?)   (I trust Him fully.)

I love what Jesus does next in this passage of Scripture.

He doesn't just pull Peter out of the water, wrap him in a blanket, have a little cuddle session, and a cozy boat ride. Jesus addresses Peter's lack of faith. He's not condemning, and He's not disappointed—He simply wanted to have a conversation about it. He wanted to address Peter's fear so that the next time he faced something scary, because fear is inevitable, he had enough faith to bring him through.

Jesus doesn't want us to just keep doing this same dance with fear either. One day you're fine, the next day you're not. One year you don't struggle as much with fear, the next you're consumed with it. Jesus doesn't want you to go on another incredible date, then be full of anxiety. He doesn't want you to run away when your loved one gets sick. He doesn't want you to wake up in the middle of night and feel like He's left you.

Jesus wants to build faith up inside of you so that what might feel impossible—like walking on water—becomes possible through your trust and reliance on Him!

As you close out today, spend some time in prayer and get to the root of your fear. Ask yourself the question that Jesus asked Peter, "Why do you doubt?" Get honest, be vulnerable, and let Him in.

THE SOUR SIDE: ANXIETY

Kenz

It's probably not too difficult to guess what the sour side of fear is. Sadly, it's become one of the most well-known and normalized emotions.

"I've been struggling with anxiety lately." "Oh, same."

"Last night I stayed up all night because I was so anxious." "Been there before."

"I could barely breathe I was so anxious!" "Totally."

Here's how anxiety develops. When we're afraid, we try to control or frantically manage what is happening. But because so much is out of our control, fear leads to anxiety. An emotional, spiritual, and quickly physical spiral.

The physiological reaction to anxiety often looks like your heart rate increasing, breathing becomes difficult, your chest tightening, and feeling feverish. I've often heard that anxiety feels like an elephant is sitting on your chest.

Anxiety is real and there's no getting around that.

What has anxiety looked like in your life?

On a scale from 1-10, how extremely do you experience this feeling?

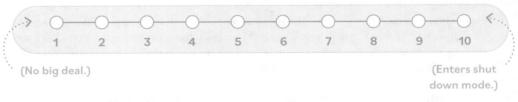

1   2   3   4   5   6   7   8   9   10

(No big deal.)   (Enters shut down mode.)

Anxiety is much more than just a physical reaction, it's deeply spiritual too. Like we briefly talked about yesterday, anxiety convinces our hearts that we don't need anyone's help, especially not God's help. In our anxiety, we cannot feel or see Him— which makes things even more scary. So what do we do? We try to control our own future in an attempt to protect ourselves from our past or future unknowns.

I've been experiencing this lately.

My sister, who's my best friend and favorite person on the planet, lives in New York City. It's fun and cute and all, but that city scares me. I truly have nightmares of her walking back to her apartment at night alone. I keep my phone next to my bed with the volume on high just to make sure I don't miss any panicked calls. I lay awake in bed at night, checking her location until I see she's made it back safely. Sometimes I wake up in the middle of the night thinking something bad has happened. My heart races, my breath shortens, and I panic.

I'm literally one thousand miles away, yet I still think that by having my phone next to my bed and keeping my eyes open that I can keep her safe, that I can control what happens to her. Crazy, right? But that's how anxiety controls us, until we let Him take back control.

There's this verse that someone's probably shared with you in an anxious moment.

> *Be still, and know that I am God.*
> PSALM 46:10, ESV

Sound familiar? Well, instead of mustering up the faith to believe this for yourself, let's dig a little deeper and look at what this really means for us.

Open up your Bibles to Exodus 13.

The Israelite people had been living in Egypt for almost four hundred years under the rule of Pharaoh. Pharaoh was an awful person and hated the Israelites. He brutally enslaved them and then ordered that all the Israelite boys be drowned in the Nile river. The Israelites, for good reason, were extremely afraid of Pharaoh.

God called upon Moses to release the Israelites from Pharaoh. God promised to deliver them and protect him, but it was going to take a while for this promise to be fulfilled.

First, God had to change Pharaoh's mind. If you ever attended Sunday school, you might remember all the plagues God sent? The flies, the boils, the hail—flip through Exodus 7–12, and you'll see what I'm talking about.

Finally, we reach the moment when the Israelites are about to experience victory. God led them to the Red Sea.

What does Exodus 13:17 say?

God knew that the Israelites were at their wits' end, and if they took the path through the land of the Philistines, they would have given up and gone back to Egypt. There was only one way they were going to get through this and that was to cross the Red Sea.

I don't know about you, but I love seeing these "small" moments when God has our backs even as we're unaware of it. God navigating the Israelites reminds me that He's always thinking and working on our behalf—that there really is nothing to be afraid of—but I'm getting ahead of myself. Let's jump back into the Scripture passage.

Stop and read Exodus 14:1-10.

Pharaoh is back on the scene! This time he's gathered six hundred of the best chariots and officers, and they are beginning to pursue the Israelites. Meanwhile, the Israelites are camped near the sea and clearly cornered between this large body of water and the approaching troops.

Fill in the blank for Exodus 14:10

As Pharaoh approached, the Israelites looked up and there were the Egyptians coming after them! The Israelites were _____ and _____ _____ to the LORD for help.

As you can imagine, the Israelites were freaking out, and I can understand why! There's no way they are going to be able to swim across the Red Sea. They are stuck and the Egyptians are about to destroy them if God doesn't do the miraculous. In an effort to control their situation, the Israelites began to ask Moses a series of irrational and anxious questions.

Stop and read Exodus 14:11-12.

What irrational thoughts or questions go through your mind when anxiety creeps in?

Moses responded to their anxiety, just like God is responding to yours. These are powerful words, so take a moment to allow them to sink in.

"Don't be afraid. Stand firm and see the LORD'S salvation that he will accomplish for you today; for the Egyptians you see today, you will never see again. The Lord will fight for you, and you must be quiet."
EXODUS 14:13-14

Just as promised, the Lord parts the Red Sea and the Israelites cross safely through it. HOLD UP! Did you hear that?

As you finish reading Exodus 14, you'll read that the Lord split the sea in half and the Israelites walked straight through it. I mean, are you kidding me? That's our God!

Yesterday, we read about Jesus and Peter walking on top of the water. Today, we're hearing about the Red Sea literally splitting in half, and I'm still over here trying to control my sister's safety via my cellular device.

I can hear the words Jesus spoke to Peter as doubt was overcoming him:

> *"You of little faith, why did you doubt?"*
> MATHEW 14:31

How do the miracles of Jesus shift your perspective on the things you're most anxious about?

It scares me to think that people are becoming okay and, even worse, accepting their anxiety. It scares me because I'm afraid of the outcome.

Think about this. If Moses hadn't spoken faith and confidence into the fearful hearts of the Israelites, they would have surrendered to the Egyptians and gone back into slavery.

Our anxiety has the power to do that same thing. If we don't address it, if we become okay with it, if we make decisions out of it, we're going to end up in slavery to our fears.

It's time to rise up in faith and take back the promises that God has placed on your life. It's time to stand firm and look at what He will accomplish for you today. He is working on your behalf. He is in control. He is behind you and beside you.

He is for you.

> *Be still, and know that I am God.*
> PSALM 46:10, ESV

THE INVITATION: FAITH

Mac

When I was in college, I had a good friend who struggled with fear more than anyone I had ever met before. Because of some traumatic experiences from her childhood, fear was quite literally around every corner of my friend's life.

For the most part, she couldn't be left alone out of fear of what could potentially happen to her. As a friend group, we would take turns sleeping over at her apartment, walking her to her car at night, and even checking her back seat for kidnappers or scary people.

Is there fear in your life that no matter how hard you try, you just can't get rid of? Name it here.

I remember talking with her on one of those nights I stayed at her house when she told me, "Mac, I know all of the Bible verses; the 'fear nots' and all the prayers I'm supposed to pray when I'm afraid, but if I'm being honest, they don't work for me. No matter how much I pray or how hard I try, the fear is still there."

My heart broke for her. I had seen her on her knees before God so many times, yet she couldn't escape the very real emotion of fear. I remember feeling so helpless in that moment because I didn't know what to say or do to comfort her.

Had God abandoned her? Where was He? Why was He not answering her prayers? Why was she still experiencing fear?

How has your experience with fear left you feeling towards God?

The truth is that fear is a very real part of so many of our lives, and I think more often than not it gets a bad rap. We feel fear and we immediately try to wish it away. But what if there's something underneath the fear that, if we pay attention to it and discern with the Lord, could be the key to unlocking our greatest strength, and perhaps even our greatest calling?

Let's open up our Bibles and look to Scripture that speaks to the invitation or the gift that we can experience from the feeling of fear.

Fill in the blanks below:

"The _____ of the LORD is the beginning of _____ ;
all who follow his instructions have good insight. His praise endures
forever" (Ps. 111:10).

"The _____ of the LORD is the beginning of _____ ;
fools despise wisdom and discipline" (Prov. 1:7).

"In the _____ of the Lord one has strong _____
and his children have a refuge. The _____ of the Lord is a
_____ _____ _____ , turning people away
from snares of death" (Prov. 14:26-27).

"The _____ of the LORD leads to _____ ; one will sleep at
night without danger" (Prov. 19:23).

Did you catch that? Maybe we should all go back and read those verses one more time just to be sure. Fear is the beginning of wisdom. It leads to life, contentment, protection, and confidence. You see, without fear, there is no true faith. Fear recognizes that we as human beings have limitations and are in deep need of a loving, forgiving, protecting, and saving God. Fear is what ultimately allows us to admit our weaknesses, cry out to God for help, and allow Him to lead us in wisdom and provide for us in ways that we could never for ourselves.

I mean think about it, all throughout the Bible and history, fear has been the catalyst to some of the biggest moves of faith the world has ever seen. When Daniel was sitting in the lion's den (Dan. 6), my guess is that he wasn't immune to fear, but rather he let his fear lead him to a deeper faith in his God.

A few chapters before in Daniel 3, Shadrach, Meshach, and Abednego were thrown into the fiery furnace by King Nebuchadnezzar, and I'm sure they felt all sorts of fear. Can you imagine standing right in the middle of a roaring fire? I would be freaking out! But despite their very real fear, they stayed hopeful and expectant of their God. And God pulled them through with not a single hair their heads singed.

Let's move on to one of my favorite stories in the Bible to see another time God showed up in the midst of someone's fear.

Open up your Bible to Esther 4.

At first glance, the book of Esther appears to play out more like a soap opera than a Bible story. It's ten chapters full of corruption, deceit, racism, ego, and violence. The story takes place about one hundred years after the Babylonian exile of the Jewish people from their land. So this story centers around an exiled Jewish community living in Susa, the capital city of the ancient Persian empire.

Before you jump into the text, let's build some context and meet the main characters.

First, we have the *King of Persia*, essentially a drunken mess who banished his wife and held a beauty pageant to find a new one. *Esther* was a beautiful Jewish woman who caught the eye of the king, and in a strange turn of events, became queen despite her Jewish identity. She was an orphan living in a foreign land raised by her beloved cousin and trusted friend, *Mordecai*. Finally, there was the evil advisor to the king, *Haaman*, who hated Mordecai because he refused to bow down to him.

After finding out Mordecai was Jewish, Haaman convinced the king to issue a royal decree to destroy all of the Jewish people. Mordecai knew that Esther was the only one who had enough influence with the king to stop this decree. Mordecai tried convincing her to go and plead the case of her people before the king in an attempt to save them. This is where our story picks up in Esther 4.

Stop and read Esther 4:10-14.

What was Esther afraid of (v. 11)?

Esther knew that she was standing in the face of very real danger. What Mordecai was asking her to do was incredibly risky. Everyone knew that if you approached the king without being summoned, you could be put to death. But on the other hand, the extinction of her people was a very real possibility, and what if the king or Haaman eventually found out about her true identity?

I'm sure that fear was beginning to bubble up inside of Esther. Was it the fear that she would disappoint her people, the rational fear that she would be physically harmed, or maybe the fear that she didn't have what was necessary to get the job done?

Mordecai, knowing that in this moment fear was unavoidable for Esther, spoke these powerful words that mark a change in her spirit.

Fill in the blanks from the end of Esther 4:14:

> Who knows, perhaps you have come to your royal position for
> _____ _____ _____ as this.

Maybe it was for such a time as this!

It's often in the moments when we come toe-to-toe with danger, when we're overwhelmed by fear, that we begin to see our deepest calling, our biggest passion, and our God-given purpose.

How might the thing you fear the most actually be for "such a time as this"? What specific calling might God have for you in it?

Stop and read Esther 4:15-17.

What does Esther decide to do in verse 15?

In verse 15, Esther's fear leads her into an act of deep faith. She turns to her God. She is so desperate for Him to intervene that she decides to fast, or go without food, so she can wait upon Him and allow His strength to be what compels her to do the very thing she is most afraid of.

What would it look like to tangibly build faith in God no matter what fears you might be facing in your life right now?

You see, it was Esther's fear that made her faith that much more beautiful, profound, and genuine. It wasn't a faith in her circumstances, but a faith in God's never-changing character. She used her fear to connect with God in a deeper way and found a new level of dependence and faith.

What's beautiful about fear is that if used well, it can actually become the antidote to worry and anxiety. While anxiety convinces you that you need to take back control, fear can build faith that gives you the trust to relinquish control to the Creator of the universe, who knows you by name and numbers every hair on your head.

Stop and read Psalm 56:3-4.

Sure, you can let fear lead you to worry, control, and anxiety. Or you can accept God's invitation in your fear, embrace what you're scared of, release control, and reach out for help from your loving Father in heaven.

Despite your fears, will you yield to His voice calling you out of the boat, onto the waves, eyes locked on Him?

| Absolutely not! | Ehhhhh, maybe. | I want to, but I'm still scared! | Yes, but kinda nervous. | 1,000 % |

LIVE IN FAITH

Mac

All throughout the pages of Scripture, we see men and women who came toe-to-toe with some incredibly scary stuff. Just like we talked about yesterday, there's Daniel in the lion's den; Shadrach, Meshach, and Abednego in the fiery furnace; and Esther before the king. But still there are others—David slaying a giant, Moses standing before Pharaoh despite his insecurities, and Mary having to tell her friends and family that she was pregnant with God's son.

One of the biggest transformations we see in Scripture of people moving from deep fear to extraordinary faith is the disciples, the twelve men who walked with Jesus during His time on earth.

On His last night with them, Jesus broke bread with them in a quaint upper room within the city gates of Jerusalem. There He left them with a few powerful words about what things would look like when He was no longer physically with them.

> *"I have spoken these things to you while I remain with you. But the Counselor, the Holy Spirit, whom the Father will send in my name, will teach you all things and remind you of everything I have told you. Peace I leave with you. My peace I give to you. I do not give to you as the world gives. Don't let your heart be troubled or fearful."*
> JOHN 14:25-27

Jesus promised the disciples two very important things. First, although He was leaving them in the way they knew, God was sending a helper, a companion, the Holy Spirit in His name to walk with them through whatever was ahead. Second, He promised to also leave them with His peace.

It was customary during this time to wish peace (*shalom*) to people as you were leaving.[2] But Jesus's goodbye had a far deeper meaning. Jesus carried peace with Him no matter where He went or what He faced. Remember Day 1 of this week when we saw Him calmly walking on water in the midst of a coming storm? Talk about peace!

And then in John 14, we see Jesus getting ready to be betrayed, turned over to His enemies, and hung on a cross to take on the sin and shame of all mankind for eternity, and all He can talk about is peace. Despite the very scary circumstances He faced, He found a way to take total comfort in His Father.

Jesus told His disciples that although He was getting ready to leave them, He was leaving them with the same kind of peace He had. This was the kind of peace that could wash away all of the worries, fears, and doubts they were experiencing in that moment and every moment from that point forward.

This is not the temporary peace we know when we light our candles, diffuse some essential oils, and drink a warm cup of coffee in the morning. It is a supernatural peace that comes from the Holy Spirit living within you.

With your group, lean into what it looks like to walk with spiritual peace in the midst of your deepest fears. Pray for God's supernatural and inexplicable peace over every scary situation that your group is facing.

OPEN IT UP:

1. **Which of the eight core feelings are you feeling the most at this moment?**

Hurt   Lonely   Sad   Anger   Fear   Shame   Guilt   Joy

2. **When you were a child, what was the thing that you were most afraid of?**

LET'S GET REAL:

1. What's your deepest fear? The thing that keeps you awake at night? Get as real, descriptive, and vulnerable as possible.

2. How have you seen this fear turn into anxiety? What does anxiety typically look like for you?

LIVING INTO THE INVITATION:

Faith isn't the magical fix-all to your fears, but rather, it is what surfaces when you trust God in the very face of your fears. Hebrews 11 is often referred to as the "Faith Hall of Fame." In it, the writer introduces us to men and women from the Old Testament who believed in God and pursued His promises despite their circumstances.

Stop and read Hebrews 11 together, then discuss the following questions:

1. What are a few connections between faith and fear for some of the people listed in this chapter?

2. How can you begin to tangibly face your fears with God? What would this look like for you?

GIVING THE INVITATION:

Jesus walked in peace because He is the Prince of Peace (Isa. 9:6). I can imagine a wave of peace followed Him everywhere He went. You know that friend who's presence alone makes you feel better or the comfort of your mom taking care of you when you're sick? That's how I imagine it was like to be around Jesus.

But what would it take for us to live like Jesus and be the carriers of peace for our friends and family?

1. If you're being honest with yourself, how have you not been a carrier of peace? In what ways or areas of life have you possibly been the catalyst or cause of someone else's anxiety?

2. How can you begin to be a carrier of Jesus's peace? What should that tangibly look like in your relationships on a regular basis?

WHEN I'M FEELING ASHAMED

WEEK 6

LISTEN

Scan the QR code below to join us for a podcast conversation all about shame. We will share more about how we see shame present in the world around us, how it has affected our own lives, and how we're learning to process it with Jesus in a new, healthy way. We're so excited to process the feeling of shame with you this week.

THE CORE FEELING: SHAME
Mac

Shame.

It's one of those words that can feel dirty just saying it out loud. The word alone can make us want to cower away and retreat into the shadows of our brokenness. We've been taught from an early age to do everything we possibly can to avoid the feeling of shame. Because why would we ever want to feel it?

Shame has often been the voice that has distorted our identity and convinced us that we're unworthy, not enough, or too messed up to ever be a recipient of someone else's love—let alone our perfect and holy God's.

We've been indoctrinated to feel the heavy weight of shame with no one to help us carry the nasty burden it leaves. We've all been the recipients of these common phrases and have even uttered them ourselves.

+ Shame on you.
+ The walk of shame.
+ Fool me once, shame on you. Fool me twice, shame on me.
+ You ought to be ashamed of yourself!

All of these phrases purposely invoke the feeling of shame. Feeling shameful about things we've done, said, or failed to do has become as easy and natural to us as tying our shoes. It's second nature response that injects hurtful messages of deceit into our hearts that define us as defective, inadequate, or too far gone.

Maybe shame entered your story when you experienced traumatic abuse and you feel that you're dirty and can never be made pure again.

Maybe your shame stems from those hurtful comments that consistently whisper to you that you're ugly and will never be beautiful until you lose the weight.

Maybe you've been feeling ashamed of the fact that you accidentally accumulated an insane amount of credit card debt throughout college.

Maybe your shame is from that sin pattern that you can't escape no matter how hard you try. You constantly feel pathetic and mad at yourself for failing again.

Perhaps you feel ashamed of your life every time you scroll through social media and see all of your friends' successes and accomplishments. You feel that all you've been able to do is scrape by with less than average grades and a nasty bout of anxiety.

Shame takes on a million different shapes, but it never fails to convince us that there is something innately wrong with us that we need to keep hidden away from the world.

How familiar are you with the feeling of shame on a scale from 1-10?

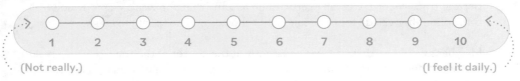

| 1 | 2 | 3 | 4 | 5 | 6 | 7 | 8 | 9 | 10 |

(Not really.)   (I feel it daily.)

What's something from your past or present that you're currently experiencing shame in?

Let's open up our Bibles together and turn to John 4 to read a story about an encounter between Jesus and a woman who was all too familiar with the crippling weight of shame in her life.

Stop and read John 4:1-8.

According to verse 6, what time of day was it?

Who else showed up to the well in verse 7?

An unnamed Samaritan woman showed up at the well to draw water while Jesus was there. It was the hottest part of the day when the sun was at its highest point. At first glance, this might seem totally normal, but this was a very unusual time for a woman to be collecting water—not to mention she came to the well alone. Typically, women would travel in groups and would only go during the cool of morning when the heat was far less intense.[1]

It seems that there is something strangely off about this woman. Why was she alone? Why would she purposely go to the well at the hottest part of the day? What was she up to?

Stop and read John 4:9-18.

What does verse 18 tell us about this woman?

Jesus knew that this woman had been in five different marriages, and the man she was living with at the time wasn't even her husband. This woman had a less than perfect track record. We can pretty much assume that she was a woman known all throughout her village for her scandalous choices and her past mistakes.

My guess would be that she was constantly at the center of the town gossip. I'm sure she heard her name in the whispers of the townspeople she passed by. I bet she felt their judgmental stares on her back as she went about her daily errands throughout the village.

This all starts to make sense as to why she was drawing water from the well during the heat of the day. She was running away from her shame! She would likely stop at nothing to avoid feeling any more ashamed of herself than she already did.

When you feel the emotion of shame, how do you typically respond?

A) I ignore it and pretend like it's not there.

B) I run away and avoid my relationships with family/friends and God.

C) I feel overwhelmed by it and feel stuck/hopeless.

D) I confess it quickly among trusted relationships.

Her shame had convinced her that she was better off alone, safe among the dark shadows of her brokenness, hidden away from any prying eyes, and removed from any reminders of her shame—at least until Jesus showed up.

One random afternoon, a strange but kind Jewish man showed up at the well, asked her for a drink of water, and then told her everything she had ever done. He knew her deepest, darkest secrets, everything she was ashamed of, all the junk that she was so afraid to reveal, and rather than condemning her, Jesus offered her living water.

Like what? Jesus didn't bat an eye at her past. He didn't see her as the rest of her village saw her. He saw her as the perfect candidate for His forgiveness, love, grace, and redemption.

You see, that's what Jesus sees when He looks at you and the shame you've been tirelessly carrying around for years.

He doesn't bat an eyelash at your failures, your mistakes, or your past sins. He doesn't see you as impure, not enough, or too far gone. Jesus stands ready with open arms for you to step into His invitation of grace and transformation. When Jesus looks at you, He is not ashamed of you. He isn't embarrassed to call you His, and He doesn't see the weight of your past. He looks at you and sees His beloved daughter for whom He is calling into a new future.

Stop and read Zephaniah 3:14-17.

Write down some truths from these verses that your heart needed to be reminded of today.

Now sit with Jesus for a moment and let those words from Zephaniah 3 be the medicine for your shame. Let them sink deep within your heart as you realize that God takes great delight in you, regardless of your past, regardless of your failures, and regardless of any misconstrued identity that toxic shame has tried to attach to you.

Jesus brings peace to your heart with His love. He removes any judgment that has come against you. He rejoices over you with His song.

Do you believe that?

| There's just no way! | I want to but my shame is too heavy. | Ehhhhh, maybe on some days. | Yes, but I still have a few doubts. | 1,000 % |

This week, we're going to confront all of the shame in our lives head-on at the feet of Jesus. We're going to see how so many of our experiences with shame have turned sour, and how we can step into the invitation from Jesus to surrender our shame. Whenever the heavy voice of shame tries to lure you back in with its lies, turn back to Zephaniah 3 and let those words wash over your heart again and again.

THE SOUR SIDE: SELF-REJECTION

Mac

Feeling ashamed isn't a new thing. It's not something that started in our parent's or grandparent's generation, or burst onto the scene when social media became a thing. No, it's been around since the very beginning. The first two people to walk upon this earth felt the raw and real emotion of shame. That's right—the apple eating, garden living, naked, walking with God, original power couple—Adam and Eve felt ashamed.

We talked a little bit about Adam and Eve back in Week 2, but maybe it has been awhile since you've read Genesis in depth, so let me give you a quick recap. In Genesis 1, God spoke the world into existence—the sun, moon, stars, oceans, rivers, creatures of the land and sea, and finally mankind. God created Adam and Eve in His own image then gave them dominion over every living thing. Seeing that His work was "very good," God finally rested on the seventh day.

In Genesis 2, we get a more thorough look at the creation of mankind.

Stop and read Genesis 2:4-25.

Okay, that was a lot but let's recap all together. When God created Adam, He created Adam from the dust of the earth and breathed life into his lungs through his nostrils. God then gives Adam only one guideline for life with Him in the garden.

What's the command God gives Adam in verse 17?

He tells Adam that he can eat from any tree in the garden except for one: the tree of the knowledge of good and evil. (More on this later!) God then invited Adam to help him name all of the animals, birds, fish, and every living creature on planet earth. Can you just imagine God and Adam doing this? I'm sure they lol'd at what to call platypuses and naked mole rats. I bet they thought sloths were the cutest things ever and I'm sure it took days to properly name every single living creature out there.

In verses 20-21, we find out that of all the animals God created, none were a suitable helper for man. So God put Adam to sleep and created Eve from one of Adam's ribs. God brings Eve to Adam and he is overjoyed, so much that he starts spouting off poetry about how great she is and what he's going to call her. Finally in the last verse of Genesis 2, we read a pretty profound statement.

Complete the verse from Genesis 2:25 below:

> "Both the man and his wife were _____,
> yet felt no _____."

They were naked and felt NO shame. Now remember that this was before the fall, meaning sin had yet to enter the world. I want you to picture this for a moment. Okay, hold up. Please don't picture Adam and Eve physically naked, but picture what their relationship with God was like.

Their nakedness meant that they were totally open and exposed before God and each other. They had nothing to be ashamed of, nothing to hide, and the idea of keeping anything from God had never even entered their minds and hearts. There was no striving, hiding, or covering. It was just a beautifully transparent friendship with God the Father.

Stop and read Genesis 3:1-6.

Genesis 3 is when things started to go haywire. The enemy entered from stage left and began to whisper lies of deceit against who God was to Adam and Eve. Now as someone with an extreme fear of snakes, I don't think it's by any accident that the devil chose to show himself through a serpent. (All of y'all with snakes as pet—I'm worried about you!) The serpent appeared to Eve and began to make her question God's voice and command about not eating from the tree of the knowledge of good and evil.

Satan is a pro at this. He tries to tempt us into straying from God's love and commands by getting us to think:
+ Did God really say that?
+ Does God actually know best?
+ God's holding something back from you. Go and get it yourself.

The enemy will always try to distort God's voice in your life and send you into a spiral of doubt and confusion about who God is, who He says you are, and what He's called you to. This is where shame begins to turn sour and become self-rejection. The enemy starts to attack your identity and how you see God, thus changing how you see yourself.

As we can tell from Eve's story, Satan's schemes often work! God had given Eve access to an abundance, yet she fixed her eyes on the one thing God had asked her to refrain from. Satan used that to get her to believe that God didn't have the best in mind for her, so she ate the apple and then convinced Adam to do the same.

Suddenly, their eyes were opened and everything was different!

Can you think of a time in your life when the enemy convinced you that God didn't have the best in mind for you? What was the thing he got you to believe that God was withholding from you?

Fill in the blanks from Genesis 3:7 below:

> "Then the eyes of both of them were opened, and they knew they were _____; so they sewed fig leaves together and made _____ for themselves."

This verse stands in total contrast to Genesis 2:25. Shame had now entered the story of human history. Adam and Eve's knee-jerk reaction to their shame was to first cover themselves then to run and hide. They allowed shame to turn toxic and distort the true narrative of God's heart for them.

Adam and Eve saw their nakedness, their sin, their shortcomings. But rather than running towards God to be their help, they chose to run from Him, thus rejecting their identity as God's kids in need of His grace.

Stop and read Genesis 3:8-10.

Complete the verse from Genesis 3:9

> The LORD God called out to the man and said to him, "_____ _____ _____?"

We might be quick to think that those three words carried a tone of angry interrogation from a displeased God, but knowing His goodness, we can assume that His "where are you?" was filled with love and compassion rather than anger and disappointment. It was the cry of a Father simply looking for His missing kids.

God didn't run from Adam and Eve when they sinned. Instead, He went out of His way to come looking for them. It was man who tried to run from God, man who put up the wall, man who tried to cover himself before going to God in his shame.

But God never stopped pursuing.

It's the same for us when we feel shame. We are quick to believe the lie that we are a mistake and God wants nothing to do with us. Therefore, we think we must run and hide or cover our sin before coming back to Him. But that's not God's heart for us!

Think back to the last time you messed up, disobeyed God, or did something you knew was a mistake. What was your initial response?

Regardless of what you've heard or believed about God in the past, let Adam and Eve's story remind you that the very second you mess up, God comes pursuing. Nothing from your past, no addiction, no choice you made last week, no website you looked at, no painful experience from your childhood, no sin pattern you can't break, and no lie of the enemy can separate you from God's lavish love for you.

Fill in the blanks from Romans 8:38-39 below:

> For I am persuaded that _____ death nor life, nor angels
> nor rulers, nor things present nor things to come, nor powers, nor
> height nor depth, nor any other created thing will be able to
> _____ us from the _____ of God that is in
> Christ Jesus our Lord.

Adam and Eve's shame drove them to believe lies about God's love and convinced them that they needed to cover their nakedness with fig leaves. When shame turns sour, we attempt to take things into our own hands by trying to earn everything by our own merit. Shame in its most extreme and toxic form tells us that if we show people who we really are, we will always be rejected. That leads us to hiding and covering up who we truly are.

But God always wanted us to be unashamed before Him. That's God's heart for you! When you mess up or fall short, rather than masking what's really in your heart, He wants you to call out to Him.

What keeps you from calling out to Him? How would it look for you to be vulnerable before God right now?

God's heart for you and I in our shame is shown all throughout the Bible. The second we mess up, He's not mad, but He comes in close. God proved just how badly He wanted to meet us in our sin and shame by sending His Son Jesus to die a painful death on the cross so that we might choose to come running back to Him.

The next time that toxic shame tries to convince you that you need to run and hide, listen for God's voice calling out: "Daughter, where are you?"

You don't have to hide from Him, you don't have to clean yourself up first, you don't have to reject who you are. God is extending an invitation underneath the shame you're feeling. Will you surrender to His voice today?

THE INVITATION: HUMILITY

Kenz

As you know by now, Mac and I started a college ministry together when we were sophomores at Belmont University. At first, it was just a small group of girls gathering together on our campus to study the Bible, learn from each other, grow together, and keep each other accountable in that crazy season of life. But then this Bible study started to grow and there were almost a hundred women showing up every single week!

As exciting as it was, it was also a bit nerve-racking for me. I had just given my life to the Lord a couple years prior and felt super behind when it came to my knowledge of Scripture or any spiritual advice. I definitely didn't feel capable of leading the Bible study conversations. When it was my week to lead, I practically had a panic attack.

I carried so much shame—the shame of not feeling good enough compared to the other leaders. The shame of not being smart enough. The shame of not being spiritual enough.

Have you ever felt shame like this before? Share your experience below.

I remember thinking that at any moment my lack of spiritual maturity was going to be exposed and someone would tell me not to lead anymore, or even worse, to stop showing up.

It all came to a tipping point when a sweet girl pulled me aside after Bible study one day. She asked if I could grab coffee with her sometime as she was going through something tough and would love some direction.

I know this sounds crazy, but I panicked! Of course, in the moment I was cool and collected, but on the inside, I felt so insecure. I didn't have any good advice and the pressure to come up with something helpful felt exhausting. No joke, this coffee date haunted me all week long.

Moments before we were supposed to meet up, I decided to stop at the prayer chapel on campus to sit with the Lord for a bit. I can remember walking in those doors with my mind racing and feeling so insecure. I knelt down on my knees, closed my eyes, and waited to hear from God. I didn't have anything to say, I didn't know what to do, all I knew was that I needed Jesus.

I don't know about you, but this bleeding woman inspires me to be more honest and open about the things I'm most ashamed of. To stop caring so much about what other people think and to care more about my encounter with Jesus.

For you, this might look like getting more honest with your friends about the things you're most ashamed of. Maybe you've been partially vulnerable, but you know there's a lot more that you could share.

This might look like responding to the invitation given at the end of your next church service or responding unashamed in worship. You've let your pride get the best of you, so you always stay in your seat or keep your hands down because you're so nervous about what others might think.

This might look like getting on your knees in prayer more often than you have. Maybe you've created such a habit of doing everything independent from God that the thought of asking Him for help actually scares you.

As you think about the current shame you're facing, what do you want your next steps to be? How can you humbly walk in the invitation God is extending to you?

Our shame has a lot of power—either the power to draw us near to God or the power to draw us away from God. As we wrap up this week's study, my prayer is that it draws you near to Him in the same vulnerable way as the bleeding woman.

And as you draw near to God, I pray that you become more comfortable getting on your knees in public, asking for prayer from your friends, opening up about the things you are most embarrassed of, and becoming a lot more okay with walking humbly before Him.

LIVE IN HUMILITY

Kenz

As we learned this week, shame has a sneaky way of distorting our identity. It's the voice of the enemy whispering lies that we aren't good enough, that we're a mistake, that our sins are too big, and that we're not capable or equipped. But all the while Jesus is trying to tell us the complete opposite. That because of Him we are enough, that we're His perfect creations, that there's no mistake too big for grace, and that in our weaknesses He is strong.

Take a moment and jot down the lies that you have been believing about yourself:

Now I want you to cover those lies with the truth—truth found in the Word of God. Below are a few verses that speak to your identity as Christ's daughter. As you read through these verses, take note of how this changes the way you view yourself, your identity, and the beautifully unique way that God created you.

> *But you are a chosen race, a royal priesthood, a holy nation, a people for his possession, so that you may proclaim the praises of the one who called you out of darkness into his marvelous light. Once you were not a people, but now you are God's people; you had not received mercy, but now you have received mercy.*
> 1 PETER 2:9-10

> *"I will bless the LORD at all times; his praise will always be on my lips. I will boast in the LORD; the humble will hear and be glad. Proclaim the LORD's greatness with me; let us exalt his name together. I sought the LORD, and he answered me and rescued me from all my fears. Those who look to him are radiant with joy; their faces will never be ashamed. This poor man cried, and the LORD heard him and saved him from all his troubles. The angel of the LORD encamps around those who fear him, and rescues them."*
> PSALM 34:1-7

So then, brothers and sisters, we are not obligated to the flesh to live according to the flesh, because if you live according to the flesh, you are going to die. But if by the Spirit you put to death the deeds of the body, you will live. For all those led by God's Spirit are God's sons. For you did not receive a spirit of slavery to fall back into fear. Instead, you received the Spirit of adoption, by whom we cry out, "Abba, Father!" The Spirit himself testifies together with our spirit that we are God's children, and if children, also heirs—heirs of God and coheirs with Christ—if indeed we suffer with him so that we may also be glorified with him.

ROMANS 8:12-17

Then God said, "Let us make man in our image, according to our likeness. They will rule the fish of the sea, the birds of the sky, the livestock, the whole earth, and the creatures that crawl on the earth." So God created man in his own image; he created him in the image of God; he created them male and female."

GENESIS 1:26-27

Take a moment and jot down any truths that you found in these verses that speak against the lies you've been believing.

As you move into a group this week, I want to encourage you to step into humility. Rather than pretending you are self-sufficient, independent, and have it all together, let your group into these lies and allow this community to point you to the truth.

OPEN IT UP:

1. **Which of the eight core feelings are you most feeling at this moment?**

Hurt   Lonely   Sad   Anger   Fear   Shame   Guilt   Joy

2. I think this week is the perfect time to talk about our most embarrassing moments. Share the most cringey, weird, hilariously awkward thing that has ever happened to you. Maybe it's not rooted in the thing we are most ashamed of, but trust me, we'll get there.

LET'S GET REAL:

1. What shame are you experiencing right now? What do you typically do with your shame? Have you been running away from it? Are you stuck or burdened by it? Like the bleeding women, take this time to share the "whole truth" and be honest with each other.

2. What lies have you been believing about yourself because of your shame? What is the truth that combats these lies?

LIVING INTO THE INVITATION:

1. How have you been trying to deal with your shame on your own? What would it look like for you to let the Lord lead you into humility through the thing you're most ashamed of?

We thought it would be fun to take a moment with your group to create individual identity statements. This is a simple statement that combats the lies that you tend to believe about yourself. Try and make it as concise, honest, and straight forward as possible. After writing them on your own, allow each person share with the group. This is the truth that you can live into!

Example: "I am full of wisdom, reflect the beauty of Christ, and am called to lead in many capacities on my college campus."

Example: "God created me to be strong and fearless. I am always surrounded by an army of angels and capable of changing the world."

Example: "My personality is full of life and joy because Jesus made it that way. He loves the way I laugh a lot and my joy is going to break chains of depression in others' lives."

My identity statement: _____

_____

_____

_____

_____

GIVING THE INVITATION:

Sometimes we feel shamed not only by the voice of the enemy but the voice of the friends in our lives. This might look like judgment or hurtful comments that might seem small at first but have the potential to leave deep wounds. We all have found ourselves guilty of this, and whether big or small, inward or outward, our words and our actions carry weight and deeply affect others.

1. If you're being honest with yourself, is there someone that you have inwardly or outwardly been shaming?

2. How can you be a part of their healing by having a conversation or healing moment with them? How can your group keep you accountable in this?

WHEN I'M FEELING GUILTY

WEEK 7

LISTEN

As you jump into this week, our prayer is that you become enlightened to the invitation guilt offers and the impact it can have on our stories. Scan the QR code and join us for a conversion all about guilt and the ways it has shown up in our lives.

THE CORE FEELING: GUILT

Kenz

Let me take you back to the first week of my freshman year of high school.

I had just graduated from the lamest middle school on planet earth (at least, that's what my fourteen-year-old self thought at the time), and I could not wait to get out of there and move on to bigger and better things.

I rolled up to my first day of freshman year in my cutest fit with freshly crimped hair that apparently caught the attention of some upperclassmen boys. They invited me over to their house that weekend, and as you could imagine, I was thrilled!

As soon as my friends and I got to this guy's house, we hopped in his car to go ice blocking down their neighbors giant lawn. (If you don't know what ice blocking is, give it a quick search. It's the Cali kids version of sledding and pretty much the funniest thing ever.) Before we hit the slopes, one of the guys pulled out his parents' bottle of tequila for some "liquid courage." Now this sheltered private school girl had never even seen a bottle of liquor and practically froze at the sight of it. One by one, they passed the bottle around, chugging and cheering each other on.

Then it got to me. "Come on," they said. "You can do it!" "Just take a sip!" Eventually, I caved and was almost immediately flooded with guilt. I could vividly hear my mom's voice telling me to stand my ground when friends tried to pressure me. I probably only took a micro sip of that tequila, but it didn't matter the amount. I knew it wasn't right.

As soon as I put down the bottle, the cops showed up. Yep, the most classic high school drama you've ever heard, right? I'm pretty sure it was just the neighborhood patrol, but either way, I thought I was about to be in some serious trouble.

Somehow, I snuck out of the car and made a run for the nearest bush. My heart was pounding as I sat there in the bushes convinced I could never leave. I probably sat there for two hours before I had the courage to call my mom to come pick me up.

Oh and yes, I hid from those guys for the next four years.

When was the first time you experienced guilt? How did you respond?

I low key wish I could hear all your first childhood mistakes and mess ups. As terrible as they are at the moment, they truly have the ability to refine and instill values within us. Guilt helps you draw lines in the sand, leads you to the people you really want to be friends with, teaches you how to say no, and reminds you of how to treat others. That's the gift of guilt.

My guilt helped me realize what was wrong and was the catalyst for change in my life. It pointed me in a new direction, created new friendships, and ultimately, led me back to Jesus. Let's just say that you didn't catch teenage Kenz with another bottle of tequila.

Have you ever thought of guilt in this way? ☐ YES or ☐ NO

It's easy to think that shame and guilt belong in the same category, but they're vastly different. Shame is rooted in our identity. It points to the lies we believe about ourselves, not in a sin that we actually commit. Guilt on the other hand is associated with our actions and behavior. It's the feeling we experience when we do something that goes against our values.

It's the feeling you get after talking bad about a friend—relieving at first, but the second you walk away, you're filled with regret. It's the feeling you get when you were a little too harsh on the phone with your mom. She made you upset, but your hurtful words didn't make you feel any better. It's the feeling you get the morning after a night out with your friends. You were just trying to have a good time, but the hangover wasn't even close to worth it. It's the feeling after you binge an entire Papa John's pizza. It was everything you thought you wanted and needed, but the aftermath is nauseating.

What do you more regularly feel guilty about?

On a scale from 1-10, how much do you carry guilt? Do you have a super guilty conscience or is it easy for you to ignore it?

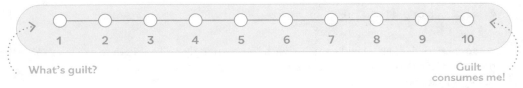

What's guilt?

Guilt consumes me!

The result of guilt has two very distinct outcomes. The first option is we run from it, deny it, or justify our actions only to leave ourselves in a prideful mess. On the other hand, we can confess it, let God use it to refine us, accept forgiveness, and step into freedom from it.

There's a story in Scripture about King David making a major mistake and experiencing some serious guilt. We are going to learn from his story how the roller coaster of emotions is something we all can face when we experience guilt.

David was honorable, lovable, and everyone's hero until his major oooooopsie found in 2 Samuel 11.

Stop and read 2 Samuel 11:1-5.

Where was David while his army was out to war?

At this point in Scripture, the Israelite army had been fighting battle after battle, so we can assume that David was getting a bit worn out. It might seem reasonable for him to take a break every once in a while, but this really wasn't an option for him as king. The Lord had placed this honorable calling on his life, and David was in no place to step back and indulge in his wealth.

What do you notice at the beginning of verse 2?

David couldn't fall asleep, so he went up to the roof to walk it out. I imagine David knew he wasn't where God needed him to be. Have you ever been there before? When you know you aren't where you should be and temptation comes knocking at your door? I sure have!

Well in this vulnerable state, David caught a glimpse of a beautiful woman bathing in the courtyard whom he had never seen before. Her name was Bathsheba and she was married to Uriah, who was away fighting with the Israelite army. Moments later, David gave into his lustful thoughts and called Bathsheba into his palace to sleep with him.

I'm sure David woke up in guilt. I can imagine he panicked a little wondering who would find out, but decided to just get up, shake it off, and move on. Until he found out that Bathsheba was pregnant!

Stop and read 2 Samuel 11:6-27.

In response to his guilt, David came up with the seemingly brilliant idea to call Uriah home from battle so that he could sleep with Bathsheba to convince everyone that was the night that she conceived.

But as you read—not just once, but twice—David's plan failed. This sent David raging into the sour side of his guilty feelings. YIKES!

Describe what happened in verses 14-16?

David sent Uriah off to battle, but first told Joab, the army leader, to have him fight in front of the biggest and strongest guys. This was a death sentence for Uriah.

To recap, the Israelite army got destroyed, Uriah died, and Bathsheba was mourning his death. In an effort to clean up the situation, David decided it was best to marry Bathsheba, but the chapter ends with a very heavy statement.

Fill in the blank below from 1 Samuel 11:27:

". . . the Lord considered what David had done to be_____."

The truth is you can cover up your sins all you want, you can keep lying about that thing you did, you can pretend it never happened, you can share only half the truth, but your Father always sees and knows the whole truth.

Where have you been taking your sin recently?

> A) I've been telling half of the truth.
>
> B) It's sent me into a spiral of sin.
>
> C) I've brought it before God.
>
> D) I've been hiding from God, but share with friends.

I don't know if you noticed, but God wasn't mentioned throughout this entire chapter. However, we know He witnessed every little detail. God—being rich in mercy—didn't just throw His hands up and give up on David then and there. We know David's story wasn't over.

Stop and read 2 Samuel 12:1-15.

You see, that's all it takes. Just one moment of confession and forgiveness and David's whole story changes. There were horrible consequences for his actions, but God still wanted to use him. He wanted to continue to build generations of men who were strong and courageous. He wanted to restore his identity and continue his purpose.

Like David, we're all sinners. We're going to mess up, we're going to make mistakes, and we're going to come face to face with guilt. It's inevitable. The question is, what are you going to do with that guilt?

THE SOUR SIDE: PRIDE

Kenz

Yesterday, we looked at the story in 2 Samuel 11 when David experienced some serious guilt after sleeping with Bathsheba. David's first response to his guilt is what we're going to talk about today: *pride*.

Have you ever made a mistake, experienced guilt, and then totally denied the sin?

☐ YES!   ☐ NEVER!

I sure have! Let me just tell you, it's my first year of marriage and I have made plenty of mistakes. Some might say that your first year of marriage is a humbling experience, but I think I'm still learning the humbling part. The theme of my first year of marriage has been pride.

It's rare (very rare) that I admit when I'm wrong. I'll verbally attack my husband, Josh, because of the smallest mistake and hardly back down. In my eyes, it's always his fault. "He's younger than me and just has a lot of room to grow. He's the one that woke up like that. He's the one that did that. He's the one that . . ." My default is pointing my finger at him and rarely admitting to anything myself.

Oh, but when he tries to call me out on something, my pride hits it's ultimate peak and sends me into rage mode. I can relate to David making death sentences because I've considered it myself. Okay, not really, but yes, I've let my guilt turn into a whole lot of pride.

Let me clarify—I am not proud of this. The morning after a marriage battle, I'm exhausted. My pride doesn't bring me, or Josh, or our marriage any kind of joy or healing. It's purely destructive.

Proverbs 16:18 says, "Pride comes before destruction, and an arrogant spirit before a fall."

The Hebrew word for destruction is *sheber,* which describes "fractured, crushed, or shattered."[1] That sounds a lot like my pride. It doesn't build up my marriage, it fractures it. It doesn't uplift Josh, it crushes him. It doesn't restore our love, it shatters it. That's what pride does.

Pride creates a self-centered mentality, protecting our own reputation rather than caring for others.

Can you picture this in your own life? You make a mistake, even the smallest mistake, and feel guilty for it. But rather than admitting you were wrong, you decide it's best to protect yourself by denying your sin. I don't know where it goes from here for you, but I'm sure you can see a pattern of destruction. It never ends well.

Describe a time when you felt guilty, yet continued to live in denial over your sin.

Here's the real kicker, our pride denies our hearts' need for relationship with others and for relationship with God. It convinces us that we don't need His help, we don't need friendship, and we don't need forgiveness. Pride is like a big fat wedge between us and Jesus.

When I think of some guilty people in Scripture that have let their guilt turn into pride and hindered an authentic relationship with Jesus, I think of the Pharisees. The Pharisees lived in constant denial and never wanted to admit their need for a Savior, even though they needed Him desperately. They were eye-witnesses to so many of the miracles of Jesus, such as when He healed people and multiplied food right in front of their eyes. But they still didn't want anything to do with Him. The Pharisees were stuck in their ways, and they let their pride get the best of them.

There's a passage in Luke when Jesus told a parable about the Pharisees' pride, and I think we can all learn a lot in this ourselves. Let's dive in!

Stop and read Luke 18:9-14.

Jot down some initial thoughts about the way the Pharisee prayed and then how the tax collector prayed:

Pharisee	Tax Collector

Verse 11 says that the Pharisee "was standing and praying like this about himself." Other translations say that the Pharisee "stood by himself and prayed" (NIV). All this to say, the Pharisee wasn't connected to God, he was looking at himself. His prayer life was all about him.

Then the Pharisee went on thanking God that he wasn't like others in complete denial of his own sin and praising himself for all his good deeds. Crazy, right?

Then there's the tax collector that doesn't even feel worthy of being in Jesus's presence. He recognized that he was a sinner who needed the mercy of God.

Fill in the blanks from Luke 18:13:

> "But the tax collector, standing far off, would not even raise his eyes to heaven but kept _____ _____ _____ and saying, 'God, have mercy on me, _____ _____!'"

The phrase "striking his chest" sounds pretty intense, but the idea behind it was that the tax collector was so aware of his sin that he hit at his own heart as a punishment. He was well aware of his shortcomings and desperate for Jesus.

The parallel is important to recognize. Although, you might not want to put yourself in the first category as the Pharisee, a lot of us are there—including myself. You've been living in pride, and your prayer life might be a small reflection of it.

Maybe you've been coming before the Lord with your own agenda. You're asking Him to intervene, but low key manipulating things on your own. You're making time for Him, but there's still that sin you're too scared to surrender or something of your past that you aren't willing to let go of. Maybe you've been coming before the Lord thinking about yourself instead of others. You've got your laundry list of needs, but they're all about you and not about the kingdom of God.

How do you want the parable of the Pharisee and the tax collector to impact your prayer life? What are some action steps you need to take this week?

You see, our pride literally blocks the Spirit of the Lord from intervening in our lives. We can get on our knees all we want, but if we are still stuck in our pride, it's just not going to work.

Because of this, some of us have even defaulted to self-forgiveness in an attempt to make ourselves feel better about something we did. We're literally making ourselves god rather than humbly restoring a relationship with our Father. We become self-sufficient rather than desperately dependent on our Creator.

If you're being honest with yourself, do you think your pride is getting in the way of your relationship with Jesus? Explain why or why not.

How can you surrender your pride to Jesus today?

The other day I was watching an episode of *Survivor* as it got down to the final three. (All of which were girls, btw. Pretty epic, right?) Well, in true *Survivor* show fashion, one of the girls had been lying and manipulating and trying to make her way to the top, but nothing was working. She was losing badly! Everyone had alliances behind her back, she hadn't won any physical competitions, and she didn't have a back-up plan. Yet every time they interviewed her on her own, this girl was one hundred percent confident she was about to win. Talk about guilt turning into pride turning into complete denial!

Everyone I was watching it with was dying laughing and saying, "This girl is totally delusional! Why can't she see this herself?" As I sat back listening to all their comments, I thought to myself, *Do I come off like that? Have I grown totally unaware of my shortcomings? What am I telling myself that might be far from the truth?* Honestly, it was an oddly humbling moment. It feels like I can go months stuck in my pride and be totally unaware of it.

The truth is, it can be so easy to forget our desperate need for Jesus. Like the Pharisee and the girl on *Survivor* (lol), we can often be totally delusional of the sin in our lives and what we need to lay at the feet of Jesus. As we close out today, I want you to ask yourself three hard questions.

How have I been running from my mistakes and shortcomings?

What sin in my life have I been oblivious of?

Do I have the courage to expose my actions in truth and vulnerability? If so, what does that need to look like?

My prayer is that you learn to surrender and step into what we're going to be talking about tomorrow—forgiveness. Our guilt can bring us into freedom and be the gift that restores our relationship with our Father.

Are you ready for that? I hope you just shouted out loud, "YES!"

THE INVITATION: FREEDOM

Mac

Three days later and I know, I know, we're still talking about guilt! Anybody else feeling like they would rather run the other direction or scroll on TikTok than open up their Bible today? WE GET IT! The truth is that feeling guilty is uncomfortable. It's not a feeling we want to sit with for long. It's not an emotion that we're ever excited to have. It's not something we want to admit or recognize in our relationships.

But guilt, when experienced in light of the gospel, can be one of the most beautiful feelings we can embrace and accept as human beings. Like we talked about earlier this week, guilt is when we do something that goes against our values or what God has called us to. We will all do this over and over and over again—guilt is unavoidable! BUT. It's in that moment of feeling the initial guilt when we all have a choice to make two very different outcomes.

Yesterday, we talked all about pride, but there is another choice.

If we allow it, guilt can draw us into the recognition that we are flawed, imperfect people in need of grace and reconciliation. Then, guilt can lead us into confession, where we recognize what we've done and ask for forgiveness to be back in right relationship with God and the people around us. This type of guilt breaks the chains of pride and toxic shame and leads us into true freedom.

Don't believe me yet? Let's open up the Word so you can hear it for yourself. This is some powerful stuff!

> Stop and read 1 John 1:7-9.

> GUILT ⟶ CONFESSION ⟶ FORGIVENESS ⟶ FREEDOM

This is the good news of Jesus. When we feel guilty, we are invited into confession—brutally honest, messy, nothing to hide, raw, and real admittance of what we've done, how we've hurt ourselves and others. Then we ask for undeserved forgiveness, and even if we don't get it from the people we've hurt, we can always guarantee that we will receive total forgiveness from Jesus. He is faithful. He is just. He forgives all our sins and cleanses us from everything we've done wrong.

That is freedom. And it's the invitation from Jesus in our guilt!

Freedom isn't never messing up. It's not being so good that you don't even need God's grace. Freedom isn't striving to be better. It's not an escape from sin or temptation or pain or guilt. Freedom isn't about what we do or don't do for Jesus but about what He did for us on that cross.

Let's open up to John 8 and see a story of freedom lived out for a woman with plenty to feel guilty about.

Stop and read John 8:1-11.

Can you imagine how this woman must have felt in this moment? Caught in the act of adultery, one of the most intimate sins, and forced out in front of a judgmental crowd. It's more than likely she wasn't wearing much clothing, probably trying to cover up her nakedness in more ways than one. I can almost picture the tears streaming down her face and the look of fear in her eyes at this moment of excruciating public humiliation.

Notice Jesus's initial response. What does verse 6 say that Jesus did?

He bent down. Other translations say that He stooped down. Instead of responding with a verbal reprimand or correction, He simply paused and postured Himself in a position of lowliness. In a way, He got on the same level as the adulterous woman. These men were trying to trap Jesus into condemning her, but instead, Jesus met her with quiet and powerful grace in the midst of her guilt and embarrassment.

While stooped down, Jesus wrote something in the dirt with His finger. What did He write? We don't exactly know. The Pharisees kept pressing Him to respond. He straightened back up and said, "The one without sin among you should be the first to throw a stone at her" (v. 7).

Then He returned to His position tracing something in the dirt. Slowly but surely, one by one, the Pharisees and the rest of the crowd walked away. After some time, all who remained were Jesus and the adulterous woman.

This woman, who was probably overflowing with guilt, had her "get out jail free" card at that moment. Instead, she chose to courageously stay and face what she had done before Jesus.

What two things does Jesus say to her in verse 11?

1. _____.

2. _____.

Two beautiful statements that speak so much to the heart of Jesus for us in our deepest places of guilt. Jesus looked her in the eyes, spoke shocking grace with no condemnation, and encouraged her to go and sin no more. He looked beyond the obvious circumstances of her current choices and refused to acknowledge them as truth for her future.

Jesus did so much more than simply forgive her. He sent her away FREED from the bondage of her sin. And that is the invitation that we also have from Jesus when we feel the heaviness of guilt. You can try to quietly slip away and deal with the guilt on your own, or you can boldly stay and allow Jesus to speak to the things you've done.

And while I can't promise you that it will be easy, what I can promise is that Jesus doesn't condemn or lecture you about all the ways you've messed up. He listens, He forgives, He sets you free from sin, and He casts a new vision for your future with Him.

I don't think it's by any accident that the very next verse immediately following this story is John 8:12.

Stop and read John 8:12.

If you've been walking around feeling guilty and wondering what Jesus's response to your brokenness is, here it is: He says, "I am the light of the world. Anyone who follows me will never walk in the darkness but will have the light of life."

Have you stepped into that invitation yet, or are you simply medicating your guilt with cheap fixes and temporary band-aids? If you relate to that second option more, let's ask Jesus for the beautiful freedom 1 John 1:7-9 talks about.

GUILT

First things first, you have to identify the guilt in your life.

In this moment, get honest. What guilt do you need to process with Jesus?

CONFESSION

It's time to confess what you've done, said, or not done that has gone against what God has called you to. No holding back, no excuses—lay out all of the messy details here before your Jesus.

What have you done, said, or not done that has gone against what God has called you to? Who have you hurt in the process?

FORGIVENESS

After honest confession before the Lord, it's time to ask for the forgiveness that Jesus so freely offers. Sit before Him and genuinely ask Him to cover your sins, brokenness, and guilt.

Is there anything holding you back from believing or accepting Jesus's forgiveness? Name it here.

FREEDOM

The forgiveness that Jesus offers invites us to live a life of freedom no longer burdened by the chains of our past. Spend some time with the Lord letting Him cast a new vision for your future.

How is Jesus calling you to live differently moving forward?

Fill in the blanks from Galatians 5:1:

For _____ , Christ set us _____. _____
_____ then, and don't submit again to a yoke of slavery.

What would it look like to "stand firm" in the promise of freedom that Jesus has offered to you?

I'd be willing to bet that a lot of us relate to the woman caught in adultery. We're ashamed of what we've done, what's in our past, the thoughts in our mind, or how we think we messed things up. We fixate on the darkness rather than moving toward the light. But I think God is extending an invitation to us all to simply lock our eyes on the light of Jesus. His light and His voice can and will lead us out of the darkness, overpowering whatever we face.

Let your guilt lead you to Jesus.

Darkness has no hold on you. Sin will not win. You can walk with the Light of the world.

LIVE IN FREEDOM
Mac

When I was six years old, the church I grew up in hosted a tent revival. If you've never been a part of something like that, let me paint a picture for you. For an entire week every summer, the church would construct a huge white tent that sat in the field next to the sanctuary. Every night, all the families would gather in the tent for worship and singing. After the worship ended, the kids would usually be excused to go and play in the field outside while the pastor brought a message. Now mind you, the pastor was my dad, so you would think that I would've stayed at least once or twice to hear him preach. But nope, I sprinted out of that tent as fast as my little feet could carry me to go play tag with all the boys in my grade that I had crushes on. I LOVED IT! Some of my fondest memories from my childhood are of those summer nights with bare feet, fireflies, and the comforting sound of my dad's voice booming from the tent as I played with my friends.

On the last night of a tent revival, they usually bring in a special musical guest, and this particular year it was Bob Carlisle. I'm guessing many of you have no clue who that is. In the 90s, he was a BIG deal in Christian music, and it just so happened that his song "Butterfly Kisses" was my dad and I's special song. It's a sweet song that describes a meaningful relationship between a father and daughter. It was the song that my dad and I listened to on the way to school every single day.

The night of Bob Carlisle's concert, my dad told me to come and find him during "Butterfly Kisses" so we could sing it together. I quickly agreed and then ran off to find my friends to start the night's shenanigans.

To this very day, I have a vivid memory of peeking into the tent at one point and hearing the opening lyrics to "Butterfly Kisses." There were these pink and purple butterfly spotlights dancing around the tent for special effects. I considered going to the front row to find my dad, but for some reason, I turned around and continued playing with my friends.

My dad came up to me after and told me that he looked for me everywhere during our song but couldn't find me. He missed getting to share that moment with me. Something deep within my little six-year-old heart began to rise up that I hadn't felt before: guilt. I had missed an incredibly special moment with my dad because I was too busy chasing boys around just like I had the six nights before. I instantly regretted it and wished I could've chosen a different outcome.

I can't even begin to tell you how many times this moment has haunted me. It's one of the single moments from my life that I regret the most. (Not even kidding!)

But in just a few months from writing this, I'm getting married to the man of my dreams. And do you know one of the things I'm most looking forward to on my wedding day? More than getting ready, more than the dress, and even more than the super fun party—I cannot wait for that father-daughter dance.

You best believe that we are dancing to "Butterfly Kisses" and I am finally going to get my beautiful redemptive moment with my dad. I have literal tears in my eyes just thinking about it!

I tell you this story for two reasons.

First, I think it shows how processing guilt well has the power to create some of the most meaningful moments in our lives—moments when what was wrong is finally able to be reconciled and made right. My father-daughter dance with my dad feels ten times more meaningful to me now knowing what I missed the first time around. I'm not going to let that happen again!

Second, I think it shows the Father's heart toward the guilt we feel in our lives. Although my dad wished that I had been with him for that moment, it didn't change his love and pursuit of me for even a second. The next time we got in the car to go to school, he hit play on "Butterfly Kisses" just like he had all the days before. Nothing had changed between us.

If you ask him about the Bob Carlisle incident from my childhood, my dad can't even tell you about it today because his memory is too packed full of moments when I made him proud, when I curled in close, and when I told him I loved him. That's what he chooses to remember about me.

That's the Father's heart for the guilt you've been carrying around. I love the way that Psalm 103 so eloquently puts it.

> *"As far as the east is from the west, so far has he removed our transgressions from us."*
> PSALM 103:12

I couldn't go back and change my tent revival decision, but I could change what I did from that point forward. And let me tell you that in the twenty-two years since that day, there have not been many moments when I've passed up an opportunity to hang out with my dad.

The same goes for you. You can't go back and change what you've done, but you can change what you do from this point forward. Start by stepping into that invitation of freedom that Jesus wants to offer you with your group today. Get more real than you ever thought possible with the women around you about the guilt you've been carrying. Confess all the messy details, lay your pride aside, and accept the forgiveness Jesus freely offers.

Then live differently out of the freedom He so generously gives.

CORE FEELING
GUILT

SOUR SIDE
PRIDE

THE INVITATION
FREEDOM

OPEN IT UP:

1. Which of the eight core feelings are you feeling the most at this moment?

Hurt   Lonely   Sad   Anger   Fear   Shame   Guilt   Joy

2. Start off this group time by sharing all about your middle school self. There's honestly so much bonding that happens when the awkward, angsty, glorious middle school days are revealed. (Pictures are encouraged!)

LET'S GET REAL:

1. What's your earliest childhood memory of feeling guilty? What happened and how did you respond?

2. What is typically your first response to guilt? Do you want to deny it and run away, or do you feel convicted to seek the Lord's forgiveness?

LIVING INTO THE INVITATION:

You've spent seven weeks together as a group, and I think it's time to REALLY get honest with each other. Like we talked about this week, freedom begins with confession—when we get really honest about the things we are carrying guilt in. James 5:16 says, "Therefore, confess your sins to one another and pray for one another, so that you may be healed. The prayer of a righteous person is very powerful in its effect." Let's live this out this week by having a moment of confession with each other so you can begin to experience freedom!

1. What in your life have you been carrying guilt about that you need to confess?

2. Have you unknowingly been using pride to cover up some of your guilt? What does pride look like in your life?

GIVING THE INVITATION:

The beautiful thing about guilt when processed with Jesus is that it can lead us into reconciliation with those that we've hurt or let down, and even with the people who have hurt us.

1. What relationships in your life do you need to lay your pride aside and pursue reconciliation in?

2. What could that look like for you? How can your group hold you accountable in this?

WHEN I'M FEELING JOYFUL

WEEK 8

LISTEN

As we start out this final week, scan the QR code to join us for a conversation all about joy. This is such a fun one! We talk about how worship, prayer, and intimacy with God have taught us how to find true joy in the midst of some of our most difficult circumstances.

THE CORE FEELING: JOY

Mac

We've made it to our final feeling, and this is one that I'm sure we've all been excited about. This week we're going to be talking all about joy! And we're not talking about the manufactured joy highlighted in Hallmark moments, the exciting scenes from the college parties you see in movies, or the end of every romance novel when the two lovebirds finally end up together.

This is a deeper kind of joy—one that cannot be easily extinguished, that isn't built on circumstantial evidence, and doesn't always end with a happy ending. I would assume that many of us associate joy with happiness, but in reality they are two very different things.

Think back on the last time you felt happiness. What made you feel that?

Think back on the last time you felt joyful. What made you feel that?

The word *happenstance* is defined as "a circumstance that is due to chance."[1] This means that happiness often finds us. It's those moments when everything seems to go right, all is well with the world, and the credit scenes roll as the happy music bops. But because we live in the real world, we know that life goes on after the movie ends and things often start to get difficult again.

Finances get tight, he stops loving you back, you don't get the job you wanted, your parents fall out of love, someone takes advantage of you, your friendship ends—the list goes on and on and on. We often stumble our way in and out of happiness every single day, but joy is altogether different because it's something that we can actively choose to live into in every circumstance.

True joy is found when we live with our hearts open to its desires. It's the willingness to step into the invitation that Jesus offers us in every emotion. It's when we stop suppressing, running away, or hiding—thus allowing our feelings to turn sour—and instead, allow everything we feel to lead us back to the throne of Jesus, where we can receive all that He has promised time and time again.

Joy is a result of our willingness to embrace the other seven feelings in their entirety.

As a review of our last seven weeks together, fill in the blanks with the eight core feelings:

We find joy when we're willing to admit our _____ so we can find healing and wholeness again.

We find joy when we allow our _____ to actually lead us into deeper intimacy with God and the people around us.

We find joy when feeling _____ because it means we recognize and embrace how much what we lost had value and mattered in our lives.

We find joy when our _____ compels us to action paired with passion for the things that truly matter to us.

We find joy when our _____ gives us an opportunity to experience the depth of what true faith is.

We find joy when our _____ leads us to humility or the recognition of our limitations thus gives us a deeper dependence on God.

We find joy when our _____ draws us to confession and reconciliation where we receive the forgiveness and freedom that only Christ can truly offer.

Doesn't that sound absolutely beautiful and like you want to run laps around your bedroom and tell the entire world about it? But if we're truly honest with ourselves, most of us don't live with this kind of joy in our everyday lives.

On a scale from 1-10, how well does this description of joy describe your everyday life?

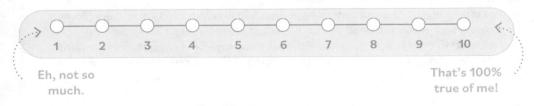

1   2   3   4   5   6   7   8   9   10

Eh, not so much.

That's 100% true of me!

Joy has become more and more elusive to us. We're used to settling for the temporary highs of cheap pleasure—the sour side of joy—to bring us satisfaction. But this kind of high always fades and leaves us feeling even more empty on the other side.

The last seven weeks together have been so fun getting all senti and in our feels, but they have been about so much more than simply getting in touch with our feelings. This journey has been about finding a way to not let our fleeting feelings dictate our love and devotion for God, but rather learning to let everything we feel be an invitation to experience His love and devotion for us fully and more intimately. That is how we get to experience the fullness of life that God created for us. It's with Him that we find ultimate fulfillment and connection.

As we step into our final week together, we want to dig into Scripture that paints the picture of joy in the midst of some of the hardest circumstances.

Turn to Acts 16 and read verses 16-24.

In verses 16-22, we see how Paul began to irritate a few of the locals when he cast a demon out of a young girl that was being used to make money as a fortune-teller. Her owners angrily took their case before the Roman leaders in Philippi causing a huge stir in the city.

As a result, what happened to Paul and Silas according to verses 23-24?

Put yourself in Paul and Silas's shoes. What feelings or emotions do you think they were experiencing?

Fill in the blanks from Acts 16:25:

> "About midnight Paul and Silas were _____ and
> _____ hymns to God, and the prisoners were
> listening to them."

Despite their dark circumstances and their very real feelings, a song of praise began to flow off the lips of Paul and Silas. That is what it looks like to find joy in every moment by allowing your feelings to lead you to the feet of Jesus. Paul and Silas could've surrendered to their fear or anger by letting it turn into anxiety or bitterness toward God. But instead, they surrendered at the feet of Jesus through worship and prayer in the unlikeliest of moments.

What's the most difficult thing you're facing in your life right now?

After their praise session in verse 25, we find that all at once, things begin to change!

Suddenly there was such a violent earthquake that the foundations of the jail were shaken, and immediately all the doors were opened, and everyone's chains came loose.
ACTS 16:26

Even though it seemed like all hope was lost, Paul and Silas chose to boldly worship God and go to Him in their lowest moment. Notice that Scripture doesn't say their chains were broken, then they worshiped. No! They worshiped first, then their chains broke. There's a huge difference.

There will be times when we find joy as God changes our circumstances. But there's a deeper and more meaningful kind of joy in intimacy with Him to be found when our world is crumbling around us and we find a safe haven in His love and grace. That kind of joy can be found in *any* moment in *any* circumstance.

What would it look like to have this kind of joy in the midst of the hardship you're facing?

Some of you right now are walking through incredibly difficult seasons. Heartbreak, loneliness, battles with depression or anxiety, relationship turmoil, financial troubles, eating disorders, and I'm sure the list could go on and on. My encouragement to you would be that no matter what you're walking through or what stage of life you're in, choose to worship Him even before your circumstances start to change.

I want to challenge you to find actual ways to worship and experience joy as you wait for God to make His move. That might look like worship in your car as you drive to school, on walks in the morning, in the back row of any church service you find yourself at, or even low-key while you go about your day. Whatever life may look like for you, use worship as a tangible way to find your hope and joy in God despite your circumstances.

What if the next time you sensed your feelings beginning to turn sour, you stopped and called out to God in prayer? What if you let Him speak to your emotions rather than Netflix, your boyfriend of three months, or your Instagram feed? God wants to offer you joy that will satisfy and sustain you further than any temporary moment of happiness.

Your feelings about your circumstances don't have to dictate how you feel about God, but rather they can lead you to find new ways to worship and connect with Him.

THE SOUR SIDE: CHEAP PLEASURE
Mac

Cheap pleasure is not only the sour side of joy, but it's oddly something we're all familiar and comfortable with.

Cheap pleasure is that delicious large pizza with all your favorite toppings dipped in garlic sauce. It brings real satisfaction while eating it, but afterwards, leaves you with a food-coma-turned-stomach-ache and grease stains on your favorite sweatshirt.

It's that all day Saturday marathon binging five seasons of the latest HBO Max show everyone is talking about. It feels so relaxing for the first two hours, but then you find yourself in a fog wondering if you even have friends or what it's like to go outside.

It's that Friday night in your dorm room with your boyfriend when it feels so good to finally just say, "so what?" and cross the boundary physically. The next morning, however, you're left reeling in a pool of regrets, totally avoiding your friends so they don't ask questions when they see your guilty face.

Cheap pleasure is that week-long vacation you've been planning for months packed full of Instagram-worthy food and drink at some trendy cafe, picture perfect poolside moments, and a chance to escape from the heaviness of your real life. But when you unpack your suitcase and start that first load of laundry, you discover that empty feeling inside that seemed to pick up right where it left off.

When's the last time you found yourself living on the high of a cheap pleasure? What was it?

Cheap pleasure feels great in the moment, but it's a temporary escape from the reality of our feelings. At the moment of it's peak enjoyment, it feels harmless, fun, and even good for us at times. That's why culture constantly tells us to "live your truth" or "do what makes you happy." And for a while, culture seems right because these things do bring pleasure, entertainment, and happiness. The problem is they always fade. The more that we use them to numb our feelings, the more broken our heart is when the high finally fades.

There was a season of my life when I was the queen of cheap pleasures without even truly knowing it. My roommate of four years was getting ready to move out to get married to the man of her dreams, my best friend's career was skyrocketing, and my sister who lived halfway across the country was pregnant with her first baby. All the people around me had lives that were rapidly changing. But it felt like I was simply stuck where I was. Could I really tell you that at the time? No, I was too busy numbing all of my feelings.

I remember so many nights when I would get back to my newly empty apartment (thanks to my roommate moving out) after working way longer than I should've just to avoid going home. I would crawl in bed with my favorite pint of coffee ice cream and start my nightly routine.

This typically involved three to four hours of Netflix, as well as texting my rotation of about three guys that I thought it was fun to flirt with, but had no desire to actually be in a relationship with. This was my coping method to distract me from my feelings.

But after a couple of months, my heart's truth became harder and harder to ignore. I was turning into someone I didn't like. I was extra irritable, physically exhausted, and more discontent with my life than ever. But because I had been using these seemingly not sinful things to numb my feelings, I couldn't figure out what was wrong. I truly felt nothing!

Have you ever had a moment when you became so good at running from your feelings that you started to feel nothing?

One night, I found myself sitting around a table at a Mexican restaurant with all of my friends and my parents, who had come to town for a visit. I remember thinking how happy I should've been at that moment, but all I wanted to do was go home and watch Netflix. And that's when I knew something was seriously wrong. I was using temporary satisfaction as a cheap substitute for the real thing to the point that my heart had started to crave "junk" more than the rich nutrients of real relationships.

Which of these forms of cheap pleasure or temporary distractions have you found yourself numbing out with? Circle 2-3 of the ones you relate to most.

Junk Food	*Movies or TV Shows*	*Sex/Physical Intimacy*
Overworking	*Shopping*	*Coffee/Caffeine*
Spa self-care	*Shallow relationships*	*Going Out Drinking/Partying*
Working out	*Social Media scrolling*	

Maybe like me, you've been there before, numbing with cheap pleasure, or maybe that's the season you find yourself in right now. Perhaps you're walking around as a shell of the person you used to be because you've unknowingly overdosed on cheap doses of temporary happiness.

If that's you, we're going to dig into Scripture together and see the story of a son who found himself strung out on cheap pleasure and the beautiful response of a loving father who welcomed Him home. Lesssssgo!

Stop and read Luke 15:11-25.

Fill in the blanks from Luke 15:13

> "Not many days later, the younger son gathered together all he had and traveled to a distant country, where he _____ his estate in _____ _____."

I had to look up what that word *squandered* means and my old pal Google told me it meant to "waste something in a reckless and foolish manner."[2] So our soon-to-be prodigal son was probably off buying Yeezy sandals in every color, gambling at the local casino, maybe sleeping around, and eating lavish steak dinners. We don't really know for sure, but we know it was foolish.

I want to judge this guy and assume that I would never do such a thing. But let's think about this for a second. I doubt many of you reading this are off spending your parent's money by the boatloads, but what about the gifts and blessings that your Father in heaven has so lavishly given you? Have you been utilizing those for His glory or for your entertainment?

Have you been squandering your relationships? Have you been squandering your time? Have you been squandering your body? Have you been squandering your influence? Have you been squandering your money? Have you been squandering your heart?

We often like to think that the prodigal son's story is just about those non-Christian people who have drifted far away from God, but I wonder if it's more of our stories than we think. So many of us are wasting the things God has given us by only feeding our hearts with quick fixes.

Any time we offer our heart a quick fix, we are essentially stopping our dependence upon God for our ultimate fulfillment. Not only that, we actually start believing that we're not even worthy of that true fulfillment that only He can offer.

In verse 15, after squandering his inheritance, the younger son has to get a real job working on a pig farm. Pretty soon, he finds himself fantasizing about the pig's food and how good it would taste just to have a bite. This sounds so crazy and absurd, but this is the narrative that cheap pleasure often tries to sell us. This was the same lie I was believing in my head thinking that Netflix by myself in my bed was better than sitting around the warm glow of a table with people who loved me.

What lies have a cheap pleasures convinced you to believe?

Eventually, the son comes to his senses and realizes it's time to go back to his father and ask if he can at least become a servant in his house. As he's on the road home leading up to his father's house, a figure starts to run in his direction. Eventually, he sees that it's his dad. I'm sure all sorts of thoughts were running through his head. What should I say? How can I convince him to let me at least live in the stable? He's going to be so mad at me for spending my inheritance! How could I be such a fool?

But before he knows it, his father's arms are wrapped tightly around his neck and he plops a kiss on his cheek. The son starts to plead his case, but before he can finish his thoughts, the father is already ushering the servants to bring the best robe, a ring for his finger, and sandals for his feet. The father actually wants to throw a party in the prodigal son's honor!

Stop and read Luke 15:23-24 again.

Many of us are like the prodigal son—so busy running from one cheap high to the other that we're almost dead inside. But the good news is that we have a Father who throws a party in our honor and celebrates our return the moment we turn around, repent, and come back to Him.

Then He invites us into His house where He shows us the riches and pleasure that only a full life with Him can offer. That's joy! It's not feeding off the world's definition of entertainment, pleasure, and happiness. It's living in close quarters to your Father and indulging in His presence alone.

Write down any cheap pleasure you need to confess and repent of today to your gracious and loving heavenly Father.

Listen, we weren't created to numb our feelings with cheap pleasures. We were created to feel and respond to the cries of our hearts alongside our Creator. I know it's not easy and maybe even unnatural from how you've been taught, but it's so worth it to experience the long-lasting, abundant life offered in Christ alone. And that true joy is so much richer than any quick dose of cheap pleasure.

THE INVITATION: FULL LIFE

Kenz

I cannot believe we've made it to the end of our time together. I don't know about you, but I'm feeling all the feels (insert teary emoji). And I want us to spend this time studying Jesus's crucifixion.

I know, I know. This is a real upbeat crowd-pleaser to finish our final session. Hang in there with me!

It is easy for me to only latch onto the second half of that story—the parts where Jesus rose from the grave, returned to the earth, is with us now in Spirit, and all is well in the world. It's the most perfect happy ending! I tend to brush past the heaviness of His death. Maybe because I didn't want to read about the gruesome murder and carry the weight of the sadness, or maybe because it feels like it all happens so fast.

If you grew up in church, you were probably told the crucifixion and resurrection all in one sitting to make sure you didn't go home sobbing to your parents. I'm sure you were relieved to hear that everything was a-okay and moved on quickly.

I wonder if some of us moved on quickly (or at least have grown numb to it all), because we've never truly felt what Jesus felt. I wonder if we've lost the sting of His death. I wonder if we've forgotten the cost. I wonder if the sadness, anger, fear, and shame of this moment were all resolved too quickly for you. I wonder if the resurrection has almost become a bandage covering up the depth of emotions that offers you the fullness of life.

Because a full life is found in the blood, sweat, and tears of your Savior.

When we fully feel what Jesus felt on the day of His death, then we will understand the life that Jesus wanted us to live. He wanted to give us a full life. He wanted us to live in freedom. He wanted to restore our joy.

If you're being honest with yourself, have you overlooked the weight of Jesus's death? If so, why?

Outside of Easter season, how often do you think of what Jesus did for you and I?

A) Maybe every couple months

B) Once a week

C) Only when we sing a worship song about it

D) Every day

E) Pretty much never

I realize this isn't an Easter weekend devo. I know this Scripture story isn't anything new to a lot of you. I don't mean to come across emo and end our time together with death. But His death, the death of Jesus, brings you the fullness life, and I don't want you to miss it!

Before we talk about His death, take some time to reflect on the life of Jesus. The crazy cool, kind, selfless, and miraculous moments that Jesus had while He walked on earth.

What stories about Jesus stood out to you over the last few weeks? (Flip back through the pages and jot down some memorable moments.)

> This is one of those moments where I really want you to lean in. So if you aren't feeling the study today, maybe you're just distracted or have something to go to, come back tomorrow. This moment should not be rushed; it cannot be sugar-coated. It needs to be felt.

There was the moment when Jesus was on His way to heal the little girl. He was becoming so popular that the crowds were surrounding Him. And at that moment, a woman with a terrible blood disease snuck up behind Him and touched His clothes. What should have been a shameful act, Jesus saw as completely different. He stopped everything He was doing, turned around, and affirmed her faith. He saw her when no one else did.

How about the time when He knelt in the dirt beside the women who had just been caught in adultery? Everyone hated her, and she probably even hated herself, but Jesus didn't want to leave her this way. He looked her in the eyes and forgave her of all she did. He was a man of grace.

There was the incredible moment between Jesus and the woman at the well, who was living in a ton of sin. She had five different husbands, currently lived with the guy she was "dating," and was practically a walking scandal. But Jesus didn't care about any of that. He saw right through her mess and offered her living water—the hope of the world.

What about the moment when Jesus sat and cried with Mary? Lazarus had just passed away, and they were mourning deeply together. Jesus, full of sadness, went to Lazarus's grave and literally asked Lazarus to walk out—which Lazarus did still dressed in his burial linens.

Jesus walked on earth for thirty-three years, and they were thirty-three INCREDIBLE years! The very last verse of the book of John says:

> *"And there are also many other things that Jesus did, which, if every one of them were written down, I suppose not even the world itself could contain the books that would be written."*
> JOHN 21:25

Don't you wonder? What were those other miracles? How many more healings and resurrections? What kind of people did He encounter and love and restore? I know it was more than we could even begin to imagine!

But while Jesus came to live a perfect life, He also came to die. He wasn't much older than you and I when His Father in heaven said that it was time.

Stop and read John 17:1-5.

What stood out to you in this prayer?

Jesus would go on to pray for His disciples, then for all future believers. (Yes, that includes you!) But as soon as Jesus left the garden where He was praying, He was sentenced to death for you.

Stop and read John 18.

Write out the parts of this passage that you stood out to you more so than any previous readings.

How do you relate to Barabbas (vv. 39-40) in this moment?

We are the sinners. We are the ones who have turned our backs on Him. We are the ones full of guilt, shame, regret. Jesus was perfect. Yet He still loved enough us to pay the high cost of sin for our salvation. And what was the cost?

Stop and read Romans 5:6-8 and Romans 6:23.

As you prepare to read the story of the crucifixion, I want you to take a moment and make it personal. I want you to picture Jesus for yourself. Not what your Sunday school teacher explained, what you learned from your Intro to New Testament class, or whoever played Jesus in the latest movie or show about the Bible. Visualize Him for yourself.

Now as you read, ask God for deeper understanding and clarity about the crucifixion.

Stop and read John 19.

Jesus died a real, sorrowful, painful death. He was hated and accused of many things. They whipped Him until He was bent over and bleeding. They mocked Him. And finally, they pierced His arms and feet with nails and crucified Him on the cross.

What feels different as you read this story today?

But did you know that even though Jesus was fully human and felt all the things that you and I would've felt in those moments, He was also full of joy?

Stop and read Hebrews 12:2.

It is in the most sorrowful moment of the gospel story where we find the invitation to experience the greatest of joys. Jesus joyfully took your place on the cross. He joyfully absorbed the wrath of God for your sins. Jesus joyfully endured the weight of your sin, so you could experience the abundant life available only in relationship with your heavenly Father.

This is the invitation we find in joy—to fully know God and to experience His unconditional, extravagant love for us.

LIVE INTO FULL LIFE
Kenz

So you've made it to the end—the very last group section! Our prayer is that this time together has created deep relationships, that it's helped you better process what you are reading, and most importantly, that it's taught you to embrace your feelings because, as you should know by now, feelings are good and from God.

Not only are they from Him, but He has feelings too. He can sympathize with us on our good days and on our bad days. Whether it's when we want to give up or when we feel on top of the world, He is right there with us.

Remember back in Week 1 when we talked about Hebrews 4:15-16? Let's look at it again and see just how much richer this verse feels after our last eight weeks together. It says:

> *For we do not have a high priest who is unable to sympathize with our weaknesses,*
> *but one who has been tempted in every way as we are, yet without sin. Therefore, let us approach the*
> *throne of grace with boldness, so that we may receive mercy and find grace to help us in time of need.*
> HEBREWS 4:15-16

Let's break this down a little bit.

> *For we do not have a high priest who is unable to sympathize with our weaknesses,*
> *but one who has been tempted in every way as we are, yet without sin.*

Jesus, although He is the High Priest and the Son of God, can also sympathize with our weakness. The ancient Greek word for *sympathize* means "to be affected with the same feeling as another."[3] That's what our God does! He knows what it is like to be tempted and to battle against sin. Though He never sinned Himself, He knows exactly what it feels like to come face-to-face with temptation.

Because of that truth, Scripture says,

> *"let us approach the throne of grace with boldness."*

What do you think this means? It means that God is approachable, and we should come to Him without reservation. He holds grace and will always be an open, loving arm.

You see, the devil might want you to think that Jesus is high and mighty, unapproachable, unrelatable, and judgmental. He wants you to think that so you don't go to God on your hardest days and when you are feeling all your feels. But really, God is the best person to run to. He'll never judge, He'll never leave you hanging, and He can understand what you are going through.

Then lastly the writer of Hebrews says,

> *"so that we may receive mercy and find grace to help us in time of need."*

God is our help in our most desperate moments. When you are afraid, ashamed, sad, hurt, lonely—you name it—He will help you through it. There is no request too small or too big. He is there for it all.

I wonder if that's why Philippians 4:6 says:

> *"Don't worry about anything, but in everything, through prayer and petition*
> *with thanksgiving, present your requests to God."*

He wants you to bring everything—all of you!

As you close out with your group this week, take the time to reflect on the character of God. What new truths did you learn? Has there been a shift in the way you view God? What new things about His character have you learned? How does the fact that Jesus felt what you are feeling change what you are going through?

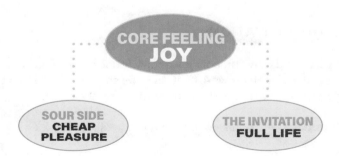

OPEN IT UP:

1. Which of the eight core feelings are you most feeling at this moment?

○────────○────────○────────○────────○────────○────────○────────○

Hurt   Lonely   Sad   Anger   Fear   Shame   Guilt   Joy

2. What has been the most joyful day of your life? Looking back, what was your joy rooted in and what was the reason for your joy?

LET'S GET REAL:

1. Is there something you're walking through right now that's simply so hard to see the joy in? What is it and how has it taken a hold on you?

2. What cheap pleasures have you been defaulting to recently? Why has this become such a habit?

LIVING INTO THE INVITATION:

Since this is the very last day, we thought it was only fitting to reflect on the last few weeks and all of the feels. As Hebrews 4:15-16 says, we should not be afraid to bring our feelings to our Jesus because He can sympathize with us in them.

1. What feelings have you experienced the most healing in?

2. What feeling brought you the most revelation?

3. What feeling is the Lord calling you to live deeper into?

GIVING THE INVITATION:

Before ascending into the heavens, Jesus left us with one final charge. He said,

> *"Go, therefore, and make disciples of all nations, baptizing them in the name of the Father*
> *and of the Son and of the Holy Spirit, teaching them to observe everything I have commanded you.*
> *And remember, I am with you always, to the end of the age."*
> MATTHEW 28:19-20

He was and still is counting on us to share the good news of Jesus Christ for the redemption of all the world. When we invite others into the gospel story, we are inviting them into an everlasting joy. A joy that isn't based upon your circumstances, but a joy that is only understood when we experience the fullness of life.

1. Who can you share this good news with this week?

2. Thinking about your week ahead, what are some new ways you can walk in and share this good news in your everyday life?

Leader Guide

TIPS FOR LEADING A GROUP

Pray diligently. Ask God to prepare you to lead this study. Pray individually and specifically for the women in your group. Make this a priority in your personal walk and preparation.

Prepare adequately. Don't just wing this. Take time to preview each week so you have a good grasp of the content. Look over the group session and consider those in your group. Feel free to delete or reword the questions provided, and add questions that fit your group better.

Lead by example. Make sure you complete all of the personal study. Be willing to share your story, what you're learning, and your questions as you discuss together.

Be aware. If women are hesitant to discuss their thoughts and questions in a larger group, consider dividing into smaller groups to provide a setting more conducive to conversation.

Follow up. If someone mentions a prayer request or need, make sure to follow up. It may be a situation where you can get others in the group involved in helping out.

Evaluate often. After each week and throughout the study, assess what needs to be changed to more effectively lead the study.

Scan this QR code for social assets to share with your group.

For more tips on leading Bible Study groups, be sure to check out www.forthegirl.com.

MAKE THE MOST OF YOUR GROUP TIME

PART 1: OPEN IT UP

You might choose to start your group with food, an icebreaker game, or just casual conversations about your week. However, when it's time to dive into the Group Time content, we have provided two prompts to help get you started. This is a great opportunity for you to lead the way (and break any awkward silence) in answering the questions honestly.

PART 2: LET'S GET REAL

Speaking of honesty, this is where you will help lead the conversation about what everyone learned in their Personal Study Days. We don't want them to shy away from being vulnerable, but you might want to ask one or two people ahead of time to plan on sharing when you get to this point.

PART 3: LIVING INTO THE INVITATION

We said this before, and we will say it again: We don't want anyone to walk away with just more head knowledge about feelings or Bible stories. Our prayer is that this Bible study will prompt real heart change as women live into the invitation that God is offering them in their feelings. As the leader, help them see the value in this section and help the group hold one another accountable in living out the truth God revealed to them through each week.

PART 4: GIVING THE INVITATION

God gives us invitations in our feelings, so we can live out His truth and extend that invitation to everyone around us. This will require another place of vulnerability from those in your group, so lead the way in how you as the leader plan to give the invitation to someone else. There may be some really cool ways you can work together as a group to serve your community, your college campuses, and your churches in response to what you learn each week.

Finally, don't forget to close out your group in prayer! You can take prayer requests if you have time, or you can start a group text where you share requests and praises all throughout the week.

SOURCES

Week 1

1. Matthew Henry, "Commentary on Psalms 109 by Matthew Henry," *Blue Letter Bible*, March 1, 1996, https://www.blueletterbible.org/Comm/mhc/Psa/Psa_109.cfm.

2. David Guzik, "Genesis 37," *Enduring Word*, January 17, 2019, https://enduringword.com/bible-commentary/genesis-37/.

Week 2

1. David Guzik, "Genesis 16," *Enduring Word*, June 7, 2019, https://enduringword.com/bible-commentary/genesis-16/.

Week 3

1. *Air Bud*, directed by Charles Martin Smith (1997; Burbank, CA: Buena Vista Pictures), streaming.

2. Strong's H5278, *Blue Letter Bible*, https://www.blueletterbible.org/lexicon/h5278/kjv/wlc/0-1/.

3. Strong's H4755, *Blue Letter Bible*, https://www.blueletterbible.org/lexicon/h4755/kjv/wlc/0-1/.

Week 4

1. David Guzik, "John 2," *Enduring Word*, December 6, 2019, https://enduringword.com/bible-commentary/john-2/.

2. Ibid

3. Chip Dodd, *The Voice of the Heart* (Nashville, TN: Sage Hill Resources: 2014), 83-84.

Week 5

1. Strong's G5399, *Blue Letter Bible*, https://www.blueletterbible.org/lexicon/g5399/kjv/tr/0-1/.

2. David Guzik, "John 14," *Enduring Word*, June 10, 2019, https://enduringword.com/bible-commentary/john-14/.

Week 6

1. David Guzik, "John 4," *Enduring Word*, February 13, 2019, https://enduringword.com/bible-commentary/john-14/.

Week 7

1. Strong's H7667, *Blue Letter Bible*, https://www.blueletterbible.org/lexicon/h7667/kjv/wlc/0-1/.

Week 8

1. *Merriam-Webster*, s.v. "happenstance," https://www.merriam-webster.com/dictionary/happenstance.

2. *Lexico*, s.v. "squander," https://www.lexico.com/en/definition/squander.

3. Strong's G4834, *Blue Letter Bible*, https://www.blueletterbible.org/lexicon/g4834/kjv/tr/0-1/.

WHAT DO YOU TURN TO WHEN YOU FIND YOURSELF IN YOUR FEELS?

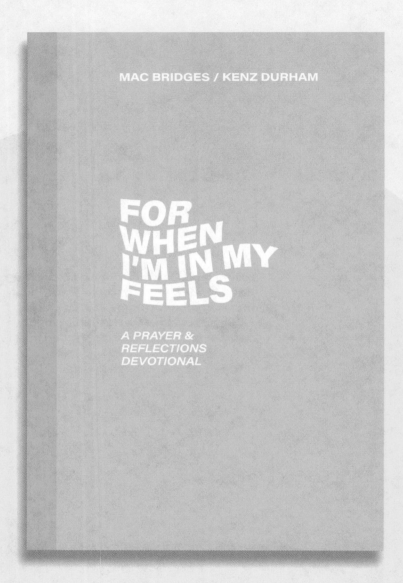

MAC BRIDGES / KENZ DURHAM

FOR WHEN I'M IN MY FEELS

A PRAYER & REFLECTIONS DEVOTIONAL

This devotional is designed to invite you to experience God through His Word and prayer no matter what feelings you find yourself in.

Grab your copy at lifeway.com/inmyfeels.

Loving this study and looking for another? Head to www.forthegirl.com for a whole bunch of other Scripture-based studies, as well as cute merch, resources, and everything you need to stay rooted in your faith. Mac and Kenz are on a mission to make sure following Jesus is a whole bunch of fun and something you don't do alone!

When Mac and Kenz were in college they started a women's community called Delight Ministries that is now found on hundreds of college campuses nationwide. If you are in college and looking for Christ-centered community, this is the perfect place for you! Head to www.delightministries.com to find your local chapter and get plugged in as soon as you can.

Get the most from your study.

Customize your Bible study time with a guided experience.

In this eight-session Bible study, Kenz Durham and Mac Bridges take us on a journey of getting in our feels together. We're going to dive into eight core feelings—hurt, lonely, sad, anger, fear, shame, guilt, and joy—and see how Scripture highlights the beauty of each one in order for us to understand and embrace our feelings.

In this study, you'll:

- Understand how you will feel and experience each of the eight core emotions;

- Discover that while all of our feelings are beautiful gifts from God, they can easily be distorted and lead you into sinful consequences;

- Embrace the timeless invitation found in God's Word that Jesus is offering to you in your feelings.

To find more Bible studies and resources for young women, visit lifeway.com/girls and lifeway.com/women.

ALSO AVAILABLE

IN MY FEELS EBOOK
An eight-session Bible study for college women

FOR WHEN I'M IN MY FEELS
A prayer and reflections devotional that provides forty days of content and helps college women navigate their feelings in light of God's Word.